"James Borishade writes with the honesty of one who has walked through brokenness and the hope of one who has discovered God's design for connection. He weaves Scripture, life lessons, and leadership insights into a compelling guide for building stronger relationships. James reminds us that our differences are not problems to solve but gifts to embrace—threads in God's divine tapestry. I have seen James live this message as CEO of Circle Urban Ministries and as a friend. His words carry authenticity and practical wisdom that will bless every reader."
Robert "Roberto" Barr, CEO and founder of Opdeployed.org

"James Borishade's book is a gift. With wisdom, compassion, and grounded tools, *Connecting Across Differences* helps us move beyond defensiveness and disconnection. It shows us how to deeply listen, speak honestly, and stay present—even when it's hard. A must-read for anyone committed to growing relationships at home and work."
Christopher R. Behrens, chairman of Circle Urban Ministries

"In a sea of self-help books, this one stands out because it places self-awareness in service of healthy relationships. With humility and grace, James Borishade combines sound biblical theology, academic insights, practical examples, and a wealth of hard-won wisdom. What a great book for couples, small group studies, and anyone open to growth!"
Donna Marsh, senior pastor of First Presbyterian Church of River Forest

CONNECTING ACROSS DIFFERENCES

SKILLS *for* HEALTHY COMMUNICATION *at* WORK AND HOME

JAMES BORISHADE

ivp

An imprint of InterVarsity Press
Downers Grove, Illinois

InterVarsity Press
P.O. Box 1400 | Downers Grove, IL 60515-1426
ivpress.com | email@ivpress.com

InterVarsity Press® is the publishing division of InterVarsity Christian Fellowship/USA®. For more information, visit intervarsity.org.

Scripture quotations, unless otherwise noted, are from the King James Version, public domain.

While any stories in this book are true, some names and identifying information may have been changed to protect the privacy of individuals.

Published in cooperation with The Steve Laube Agency.

The publisher cannot verify the accuracy or functionality of website URLs used in this book beyond the date of publication.

Cover design: Faceout Studio
Interior design: Jeanna Wiggins
Images: © filo / DigitalVision Vectors via Getty Images

ISBN 978-1-5140-1256-7 (print) | ISBN 978-1-5140-1257-4 (digital)

Printed in the United States of America ∞

Library of Congress Cataloging-in-Publication Data
A catalog record for this book is available from the Library of Congress.

31 30 29 28 27 26 | 13 12 11 10 9 8 7 6 5 4 3 2 1

Every brave soul who has ever longed

to be seen, heard, and deeply known:

may this book help you build bridges

where walls once stood.

CONTENTS

INTRODUCTION

I REMEMBER IT LIKE IT WAS YESTERDAY. The year was 1994, and I was wearing my turquoise cap and gown, feeling the weight of both excitement and uncertainty that comes with graduation day. As we neared the end of the ceremony, my name was called, and I walked across the stage. But instead of returning to my seat, I did something that caused a ripple of curiosity in the audience. Where was I going? What was I up to?

I made my way to the piano, a familiar place where I had spent countless hours, and sat down. A group of my classmates gathered around, and as I began to play the opening notes of a rendition of "Wind Beneath My Wings," the room fell into a hushed anticipation. One by one, my classmates joined in, each taking a solo, their voices distinct yet harmonizing in a way that created something truly beautiful. When we all came together, it wasn't just a song, it was a melody that resonated deeply with everyone in that auditorium.

As I look back on that moment, I realize it wasn't just about the music we created; it was about the way we came together, each bringing something unique to the performance. That experience taught me a lesson I've carried with me ever since—how the blending of different voices and perspectives can create something far greater than any one of us could achieve alone.

This lesson, first learned in that turquoise gown, has echoed throughout my life—whether as a music producer since the age of fifteen, blending diverse sounds into a harmonious track, or as a basketball coach, leading my son's team to championships by recognizing and harnessing each player's unique strengths. As the CEO of Circle Urban Ministries, I've seen firsthand how a team of individuals, each with their own talents and perspectives, can come together to create something impactful.

But perhaps the most significant application of these lessons came when I stepped into the role of CEO for the Association for Challenge Course Technology (ACCT). I was the first and only African American to hold this position, and to this day, one of the very few African Americans in the entire challenge course and zipline industry. I came into the industry at a pivotal moment, a time when many saw it as dominated by the "good old boys" club. I was brought in to bring a fresh, unique perspective, to challenge the status quo, and to advocate for change. But I quickly discovered that my voice, my ideas, often felt like a nuisance in the room rather than a contribution.

It was a challenging environment, but the lessons I had learned about the power of diversity and the strength found in embracing differences guided me. I realized that my role was not just to lead but to advocate for those who, like me, were often unheard. I leaned into my unique perspective, used it to highlight the voices of others, and fought to ensure that everyone at the table was valued for their contributions. As a result, not only did the industry grow, but it did so in a way that was more inclusive, innovative, and forward-thinking than ever before. You see, throughout all of these experiences, the lesson has been the same: harmony does not come from sameness. It comes from embracing differences.

And that's what this book is all about. I offer a perspective recognizing that the differences we often see as obstacles— whether in our marriages, our workplaces, or our communities— are the keys to creating something beautiful and enduring. It's about understanding that God designed us to be different for a reason and that by embracing these differences, we can build stronger, more fulfilling relationships.

Let me be clear: writing this book does not mean I have everything figured out. In fact, I count not myself to have apprehended (Philippians 3:13). I'm still learning, growing, and sometimes failing. A perfect example of this happened while I was working on chapter six of this book.

It was a Thursday afternoon, just a day before Dominque's (my wife's) birthday weekend. She was excited to spend Friday night at a concert with one of her closest friends. It was going to be a hot day, pushing ninety degrees, and she wanted the perfect outfit. That morning she texted me, "I need your help picking out an outfit." I immediately thought she wanted me to come upstairs and help her sort through her closet, which, by my standards, is enormous. Plus, there wasn't much time to order anything online with the concert just a day away, so shopping didn't even cross my mind.

When I got upstairs, I found Dominque scrolling through her phone, shopping online for a new outfit. I was a bit confused but went with it. A few minutes later, she tried on something she had already bought, asking me how she looked. This was my moment to shine, to give the thoughtful and supportive answer she needed.

And I blew it.

Instead of offering a compliment, I said something completely out of touch. I wish I could say I don't remember what it was, but the truth is . . . I'm too embarrassed to tell you what I said. It was dumb, and it certainly wasn't what she needed to hear in that moment. Dominque's mood shifted immediately, and the frustration was clear.

But it didn't stop there. Right after that conversation, I had to rush out to my office, leaving her stewing and upset. By the time I got to work, I knew I had messed up. I couldn't shake the feeling that I had made a simple situation much worse. So I confided in our COO—a woman I deeply trust—and asked her what I should have done. Without hesitation she said, "Why didn't you tell her to wear something like what she wore to her album release? That would have been a perfect compliment!"

I remember sitting there, thinking, *Why didn't I think of that?* How could I, the guy writing a book on irreconcilable differences and communication, not get it right in that moment?

The real test came when I got back home. The atmosphere felt thick, like a bomb was ready to detonate. Dominque was waiting for me, and she wanted to talk about my comment from earlier in the day. I remember starting off by trying to defend myself. Boy, was that the wrong thing to do. It felt like I had cut the wrong wire while trying to defuse a bomb. The timer seemed to speed up with every word I said.

Finally, I realized that what I needed to do wasn't defend myself but humble myself and apologize. I was wrong. As soon as I acknowledged that, it was like I cut the right wire. The tension eased. That apology defused the bomb.

The truth is, no matter how much we think we know, relationships require constant attention, grace, and humility. You live and you learn. Even in the areas where you're supposed to be knowledgeable, there's always room to grow. In this book I will share with you what that growth process looks like. But before we get started, let me take you back to where it all began.

It was three weeks before Christmas, a season that had always been a time of joy and togetherness for my family. But the festive decorations this year felt mocking in their cheerfulness, a stark contrast to the growing chasm in my heart. My ex-wife had moved out in mid-October, leaving our home echoing with her absence. In the weeks that followed, I had thrown myself into personal counseling and sessions with a relationship coach, clinging to the hope that understanding and change were possible. My coach advised caution, suggesting we avoid discussions of our marriage on the days we saw each other, to sidestep the landmines of past arguments and hurt feelings. I felt I was making strides, however small, toward healing and understanding.

That morning, after sending my boys off to school, the silence of the house enveloped me—a silence that had become both a companion and a reminder of the void her departure had left. Working from home had its benefits, but that day, the solitude felt more oppressive than comforting. The unexpected ring of the doorbell shattered the stillness, jolting me with a mixture of curiosity and unease. Through the peephole, the sight of a sheriff sent a jolt of fear through me, my mind racing to the worst possible scenarios involving my family's safety.

The sheriff's face was impassive as he handed me a manila envelope. My hands trembled as I took it, the weight of the envelope feeling disproportionately heavy. I can't recall if he uttered the words "You've been served," because in that moment, the world around me seemed to fall away into silence, a vacuum where time and sound ceased to exist. I numbly opened the envelope, and as my eyes fell on the summons to appear in divorce court, a sense of surreal disbelief washed over me. "Irreconcilable differences," it stated coldly, a sterile label for the myriad of unspoken words, unshed tears, and unresolved conflicts that had brought us to this precipice.

The pain of that moment was visceral, a physical ache that radiated through my chest and clenched around my heart. It wasn't just the end of my marriage that the papers signified; it was the shattering of a shared life, dreams turned to dust, and the profound grief of losing not just a partner but a part of myself. The realization that despite our best efforts, despite the counseling and the desperate attempts to bridge our differences, we had reached a point of no return was overwhelming.

I want to make it clear that my ex-wife is not a villain in this story. She is a person of depth and complexity, with whom I shared years of love, laughter, and challenges. Our journey together wasn't marred by a lack of love but by a lack of understanding and the tools necessary to navigate the vast ocean of differences between us. This moment, this heart-rending pivot in our lives, was not about assigning blame but about acknowledging that sometimes love, in its purest form, means letting go.

As I stood there alone, the divorce papers in hand, the festive lights blurring through tears, I felt an indescribable loneliness. Yet this was nothing compared to the tumultuous journey that lay ahead for my children. The grief I experienced paled in comparison to theirs—a grief that was profound and beyond my deepest comprehension. Watching their world, everything they knew and found comfort in, being irrevocably turned upside down was a sight that tore at the very fabric of my being. The stark realization hit me: there was absolutely nothing I could do to shield them from this pain.

In the ensuing days and months, the depth of their grief became evident. My attempts to maintain a semblance of normalcy, to be a pillar of strength for them, often felt like an exercise in futility. I was their coach, not just in basketball where I taught them about the discipline and teamwork needed to become champions, but in life. Yet there I was, trying to instill lessons of perseverance and victory while feeling like everything in my personal life echoed defeat. The irony was not lost on me: preaching about winning strategies on the court when my life seemed to be a testament to loss.

My children, once vibrant and full of life, retreated into themselves, becoming shadows of the joyous beings they used to be. From 2014 to 2020, until the entry of my current wife into our lives, they often went days speaking very few words, their silence a stark testament to the inner turmoil they were experiencing. It was during these years that I came to understand the profound impact of divorce on children. The notion that children are resilient and unaffected by the dissolution of their parents' marriage is a myth, a lie that minimizes the deep and lasting scars such events can leave.

I've heard people casually remark that children adapt, that they are young enough to bounce back from anything. But witnessing my own children's journey through this labyrinth of grief and confusion, I knew this to be false (at least in my personal experience). The impact of our divorce on them was tangible, a silent storm that raged within, altering their perception of stability, love, and even family.

The transformation was heart-wrenching. Moments of shared laughter and joy became rare, replaced by a pervasive sense of loss that hung heavily in our home. The resilience of children, often

touted by well-meaning individuals, does not account for the internal struggle they face, the questions they can't articulate, and
the sense of security that has been stripped away.

This journey taught me the importance of acknowledging the
deep and often unseen wounds children endure in the wake of
divorce. It underscored the need for patience, understanding,
and an open channel of communication, even when the words
seemed to fall on deaf ears. My children's gradual emergence
from their shells, their slow journey back to a place of trust and
openness, was a testament to the healing power of love, patience,
and the unwavering support of those who stood by them through
the darkest of times. This transformation was not ours alone; it
was nurtured by the support of friends and family, individuals
who became our pillars of strength, offering solace and encouragement when the path ahead seemed insurmountable.

During this period of healing, my children and I were confronted
with one of the most profound lessons of our lives: the importance
of embracing and loving our unique selves. The journey to recovery
was paved not just with the support we received from others but
with the internal realization that being true to oneself is the cornerstone of genuine healing and happiness. We learned that, to navigate
through our pain and emerge stronger, we had to be not just ourselves but unapologetically so. This authenticity became our guiding
light, a beacon that led us out of despair.

As we each embarked on this journey of self-discovery and
acceptance, a remarkable transformation unfolded. We began to
attract people into our lives who mirrored our authenticity, individuals who valued us for who we truly were and who celebrated our uniqueness rather than seeking to change it. This
newfound circle of friends and extended family members

enriched our lives immeasurably, providing a network of support and love that reinforced the idea that we were not alone in our struggles.

This process of learning to love our unique selves and being unapologetically authentic was a powerful catalyst for change. It taught us that the foundation of true connection with others lies in the courage to be oneself, with all the vulnerabilities and strengths that come with it. Our descent into despair, though fraught with challenges, ultimately led to a deeper understanding of ourselves and the kind of people with whom we wanted to be surrounded.

The emergence from our collective shell was a slow but steady process, marked by moments of joy, setbacks, and eventual triumphs. It was a journey that underscored the importance of authenticity, not just as a means to personal fulfillment but as a magnet that draws in the right people—those who not only understand our journey but are willing to walk with us, offering their support, love, and acceptance.

In this way, the support of friends and family, coupled with our commitment to being true to ourselves, became the cornerstone of our healing. It allowed us to rebuild our lives on a foundation of authenticity, understanding, and mutual respect, setting us on a path toward a future where despair has been replaced with hope and isolation with community. This journey, though born out of one of the darkest periods of our lives, has illuminated the path forward in ways we could never have imagined, teaching us the invaluable lesson that the key to attracting love and support lies in the courage to be unapologetically ourselves and expecting to encounter differences that are irreconcilable.

This newfound embrace of our differences and the warmth of our supportive community ended up setting the stage for a moment that would change everything.

The introduction of my new wife into our family's life was a turning point, an event that signaled the dawn of a new era filled with hope, laughter, and a redefined sense of what it means to be a family. Her presence brought about a transformation that breathed new life into our home, making it a sanctuary where each of us could truly be ourselves. Among the many stories that illustrate her profound impact, one involving my youngest son (now in his early twenties), stands out as a testament to her remarkable ability to connect with and bring out the best in us.

My son had a unique way of entering a room. He would stealthily sneak in, often making a peculiar sound to announce his presence without startling anyone. This sound, reminiscent of a whale's call, was his signature, a quirky yet endearing aspect of his personality. It was a part of who he was, a way for him to maintain his sense of self in a world that often demanded conformity.

On a day that now holds a special place in my heart, my wife—at the time my girlfriend—came over to our house. Anticipating my son's approach, she, having somehow picked up on this unique greeting, preempted him by making the whale sound first as he was about to enter the kitchen. The surprise and delight on his face were unmistakable. He responded with his signature sound and stepped into the room, a wordless exchange that spoke volumes. In that moment, without a word being said, he understood that he was seen, accepted, and loved for exactly who he was. The look of peace and acceptance on his face was profound, a clear indication that he felt comfortable being his true self around her.

This connection between them has only deepened over time. When my son was preparing for his high school graduation, a milestone in any young person's life, he faced the task of choosing his graduation outfit. Despite my own sense of style, he turned to her for guidance. Her background as a singer, songwriter, and actress, known for her unique and often hard-to-find stage outfits, made her the perfect ally. She wasn't just someone who could help him pick out clothing; she was a source of inspiration, a person who embodied the essence of individuality and creativity that he admired.

Their bond over something as simple as selecting an outfit for graduation underscored the deeper connection they shared—a relationship built on mutual respect, understanding, and an unspoken agreement to meet each other exactly where they were. Her influence on him, and indeed on all of us, has been immeasurable. She has become an integral part of our family's journey toward healing and rediscovery, a reminder of the power of acceptance, love, and the courage to be unabashedly ourselves. In her my son found not just a stepmother but a friend, a mentor, and a fellow traveler on the path to self-discovery, proving once again that in the most unexpected moments, we can find connections across differences that change our lives for the better.

My journey to wholeness, though worth it, was not easy. The silence after my divorce was unlike anything I had ever experienced before. Some days I would sit in the stillness and feel completely unmoored. Who was I without the roles I had come to define myself by: husband, father, provider? What was left when those things were taken away?

I had no idea who I was anymore. I remembered a time in my life when I loved singing and producing music, when the creative process filled me with a sense of purpose and passion. Music had been my outlet, my way of expressing myself and making sense of the world. But in the hustle and grind of life, I had let that part of me slip away. I had sold all of my music production equipment, convinced I needed to focus on being a "responsible" husband and father. I told myself that those dreams and passions were part of a younger, more carefree version of me and that it was time to bury them in favor of providing for my family.

I had believed that was the right thing to do. I thought it was what a good husband and father was supposed to do. But in trying to be everything for everyone else, I lost myself. I lost the part of me that thrived on creativity, that found joy in creating something out of nothing. I'd buried that passion so deep that I forgot it was even there. And in the silence after my divorce, I was left to confront the absence of not just my marriage but myself.

I would sit in the quiet house with nothing but my thoughts and wonder how I had gotten here. Who was I now? I wasn't the man I used to be, the one who dreamed of making music, of being a producer, of creating something lasting. But I also wasn't the husband I had defined myself as for so many years. I felt like I was floating in between two identities, neither of which seemed to fit anymore.

And that's when it hit me: the silence wasn't just about the end of my marriage. It was about the end of the version of myself I had built over the years, a version that had been shaped by expectations, roles, and responsibilities. Maybe you're feeling that too. Perhaps you're in the midst of a relationship that's unraveling, or maybe it's a work dynamic that's left you questioning your worth. You might even feel you're losing sight of who you are beneath the weight of it all—the person you once were before the demands of life, marriage, or career took center stage. Have you ever asked yourself, *What happened to the real me?* Maybe, like me, you've built a version of yourself that fits the expectations of the world—a version that meets the demands of relationships, family, career, and society. But underneath the person you've created to meet life's expectations is the real you, the person God created in his image. That's where we find the *imago Dei*, the truth that you are not defined by the roles you play or the boxes people place you in. You are far more than that.

The phrase *imago Dei* comes from Latin, meaning "image of God." This phrase carries the weight of an extraordinary truth: every human being bears within them a reflection of the divine. To be made in the *imago Dei* is not simply to resemble God in a physical sense but to carry the very essence of his nature. Beneath the layers of responsibilities, fears, and expectations lies the unique reflection of God's divine character placed in you at the moment of your creation. It means every one of us, in our individuality and uniqueness, reflects a different facet of God's character—his creativity, his wisdom, his love, and his justice. And this truth is life-changing because it reminds us that our worth is not contingent on what we do or how well we perform, it is rooted in who we are as image bearers of the Creator himself.

At the foundation of my identity, I was more than a husband, more than a father, more than a CEO. I was a reflection of God's creativity, his love, and his uniqueness. And my distinctiveness was not something to be hidden or buried; it was something to be embraced.

I had spent much of my life believing I needed to fit into certain roles in order to be valuable. I thought being a good husband meant sacrificing the parts of me that didn't directly serve my family. I thought being a good father meant putting my dreams on hold indefinitely. But learning about the *imago Dei* taught me that God never intended for me to erase those parts of myself. In fact, those passions and dreams were part of the way God had uniquely designed me.

In Genesis, when God created humanity, God didn't just stamp out copies of the same person. We were not created to fit into a mold. Instead, each of us was made with distinct qualities, gifts, and personalities that reflect different aspects of God's nature. God is infinitely creative and delights in our individuality. Our uniqueness is not a flaw; it's a reflection of God's divine creativity.

As I began to rediscover this truth, I started to reclaim the parts of me I had buried. I remembered what it felt like to create, to express myself through music, to build something out of nothing. I realized that those passions weren't just hobbies, they were part of my divine design. And as I reconnected with the creative part of me, I began to feel more whole, more like the person God intended me to be.

This process wasn't just about rediscovering my passions; it was about learning to see myself as God saw me. I had spent many years measuring my worth by what I could do for others, by how well I could fulfill the roles I had taken on. But God's image of me was not dependent on my performance. It was not dependent on how successful I was as a husband or father. The *imago Dei* meant my worth was inherent—I was valuable simply because I was made in the image of God. To have been created intentionally, imagined in the mind of God, and then brought into being communicates something profound about a person's intrinsic worth. It speaks *you are loved, you are wanted, you are valued.*[1]

The same is true for you. Your value does not come from how well you fulfill the roles you have taken on in life. It does not come from your job title, your relationship status, or your accomplishments. Your value comes from the fact that you were created by a God who loves you and designed you with a purpose. Your uniqueness is part of that design. The parts of yourself you may have buried, the dreams you have put on hold, the passions you have forgotten—they are all part of who God made you to be.

That's precisely why I've poured my heart and experiences into the pages of this book. Each of us carries within us our own personal narrative, a mosaic of experiences that shapes who we are and how we interact with the world around us. Whether it's in the context of marriage, a dating relationship, or the dynamics we navigate in our professional lives, the truth remains constant: we were crafted in diversity, embodying differences that were not only anticipated but intentionally designed by God.

Our differences are in fact a divine blueprint. They are threads of uniqueness that, when woven together, create a reflection of the vastness of our Creator.

So as we venture further into this exploration of relationships, differences, and the divine purpose behind them, I invite you to pause for a moment. Reflect on what sets you apart. Consider the qualities, the quirks, and the idiosyncrasies that make you unequivocally you. These attributes, these unique aspects of your being, are not coincidental. They are integral to your identity, a deliberate part of your design, and a testament to the diversity cherished by God.

Whatever it is that distinguishes you—be it your way of thinking, your passions, your approach to challenges, or even the way you enter a room—embrace it. These differences are not flaws to be reconciled but gifts to be celebrated. They are what make you irreplaceably you, a crucial piece of the assortment of humanity.

When you fully grasp that you are made in the image of God, it opens your eyes to the divine image in everyone around you. You begin to look for the *imago Dei* in others, honoring their unique qualities, their individuality, and their worth. It compels you to treat others with the same respect, dignity, and love you now understand to be your birthright. It redefines how you see conflict, communication, and even reconciliation.

This book is designed to provide tools and strategies to help us connect across our differences. I hope you'll see your own story reflected in these pages. I hope you'll be reminded that your unique qualities are essential to the melody of your life and to the lives of the people around you. Whether you're facing challenges in your marriage, seeking to lead a diverse team at work, or simply trying to navigate the complexities of your own identity, this book offers a perspective I believe can help you turn those differences into strengths. I invite you to think back to your own "graduation moment." Reflect on the unique notes you bring to the melody of your relationships and consider how, when woven together with others, those notes can create something truly extraordinary.

1

WHAT IF THERE'S NOTHING WRONG WITH YOU?

WHAT DO YOU SEE WHEN you look in the mirror?

Not physically. Beyond the clothes, the skin, the posture you've learned to perfect. I'm talking about the quiet moment when the world is still and you're face-to-face with the real you. Do you see someone created with intention? Someone carrying the fingerprints of the divine?

Or do you see your failures, your fears, your not-quites, your almosts?

For a long time I saw only the roles I had tried and sometimes failed to play. Husband. Provider. Fixer. Coach. Even now, I sometimes catch myself measuring my reflection against expectations I never agreed to in the first place.

But Scripture doesn't begin with roles. It begins with identity. Before you were anyone to anybody, you were already somebody to God. Before you were ever praised, blamed, hired, fired, married, divorced, celebrated, or overlooked, you were stamped with the image of God.

Let that sink in.

Imago Dei is not a concept reserved for theology class. It's the truth that has the power to change how you see yourself and everyone else. It means the parts of you that feel "too different" or "too much" might actually be the parts that reflect him the most.

The way you love.

The way you question.

The way you create.

The way you speak up when others go silent.

The way you notice things no one else does.

All of these aren't detours from your divine design. They *are* your divine design.

LIVING OUT THE *IMAGO DEI*

Once we understand that each of us bears the *imago Dei*, the question naturally follows: What does that mean for our everyday lives? How do the individual qualities that make us who we are reflect the divine? This is where the beauty of diversity in creation becomes clear. Each of our unique qualities—our personalities, strengths, passions, and even our struggles—reflect different facets of God's character. Together we create a mosaic that, in its fullness, reveals the vastness of who God is. These qualities are not just personal traits, they are windows into the divine nature.

Consider the quality of creativity. Those who are artists, musicians, writers, or anyone who loves to create something new are reflecting God's own creativity. In the very first pages of Scripture we see God as the ultimate Creator, crafting the heavens and the earth out of nothing. Genesis 1:1 opens with, "In the beginning God created . . ." and that act of creation continues throughout history. When we create—whether it is art, music, poetry, or even a business venture—we are participating in that divine attribute. We mirror the God who said, "Let there be light," bringing new things into existence.

For those whose gift is compassion, you reflect the heart of God as a comforter and healer. Psalm 103:13 says, "As a father has compassion on his children, so the LORD has compassion on those who fear him" (NIV). Your ability to care for others, to empathize with their pain, and to extend kindness even in the hardest situations directly reflects God's deep compassion for his people. Whether you're the person who listens patiently to a friend in need, volunteers in your community, or cares for family members, your compassion reflects God's tender care for each of us.

Those with a deep sense of justice, who cannot stand to see wrongs go unchallenged, reflect God's righteousness and justice. Isaiah 30:18 tells us, "For the LORD is a God of justice. Blessed are all who wait for him!" (NIV). You may feel a calling to fight for fairness, advocate for the oppressed, or pursue what is right even when it's difficult. This is God's justice alive in you. Whether you are working in a courtroom, leading a non-profit, or simply standing up for what is right in your daily life, your passion for justice reflects God's own commitment to righteousness.

Then there are those who reflect God's wisdom. Some people have the ability to offer sound advice, see through complexity, and help others navigate life's challenges. James 1:5 says, "If any of you lack wisdom, let him ask of God, that giveth to all men liberally, and upbraideth not; and it shall be given him." When you use your discernment to help someone make an important decision, or when you bring clarity to a confusing situation, you are reflecting God's wisdom. This gift is invaluable in relationships, workplaces, and leadership, as it brings the light of understanding into dark and uncertain situations.

Another divine quality we often see in people is strength—not just physical strength, but emotional and spiritual resilience. Those who endure hardship, remain steadfast in faith, and keep going when others might falter are reflecting God's strength. Psalm 46:1 says, "God is our refuge and strength, a very present help in trouble." Your ability to persevere through trials, to remain hopeful when the path is hard, and to provide strength to others in moments of crisis reflects the enduring, unshakable nature of God's own power.

Some people are gifted with leadership, the ability to inspire and guide others. True leadership reflects God's own authority and care for his people. In Psalm 23:1, David writes, "The Lord is my shepherd; I shall not want." God leads us like a shepherd, guiding us toward still waters and safe pastures. If you are someone who naturally leads, whether in your family, your workplace, or your community, your leadership reflects God's shepherd-like care for his people. Your ability to inspire, to cast vision, and to guide others through difficult terrain is a reflection of God's guiding hand in our lives.

Finally, some of us reflect God's attribute of peace. In a world full of anxiety and chaos, those who can remain calm and bring peace to others are a reflection of God's peace. Philippians 4:7 describes "the peace of God, which passeth all understanding." If you are someone who can de-escalate tense situations, offer reassurance in moments of fear, or simply exude a sense of calm in stressful environments, you are reflecting God's peace. Your presence can be a sanctuary for those around you, a reminder that even in life's storms, God's peace is available.

Each of these qualities—creativity, compassion, justice, wisdom, strength, leadership, and peace—reflects a different aspect of

God's character. And these are just a few examples. The truth is, every good and unique trait within you is a reflection of the God who made you. You do not need to compare yourself to others or try to embody qualities that are not naturally yours. Instead, lean into the gifts God has given you. Whether you are someone who creates, leads, listens, or fights for justice, you are living out a piece of God's own heart.

Understanding this truth doesn't just change how you see yourself, it changes how you see others. The people in your life are also reflections of God's nature, carrying within them their own unique piece of the divine puzzle. The friend who makes you laugh, the colleague who always knows how to solve a problem, the family member who always shows up in a crisis—they each reflect something of God's goodness. When we recognize this, we stop trying to mold others into our own image and begin celebrating the unique way they reveal God's character.

In a world that often pressures us to conform, the *imago Dei* reminds us that God delights in our differences. Each of us was made to reflect a specific part of his nature, and when we embrace that truth we live fuller, more authentic lives. Together we form a beautiful tapestry of humanity, each of us contributing something irreplaceable. When you begin to see yourself and others through this lens, you will not only deepen your relationships, but you will also bring more of God's character into every space you inhabit.

BUT JAMES . . . HOW DO I FIND MYSELF?

In the months following my divorce, I found myself feeling lost—disconnected not just from my marriage but from myself. I had spent so many years defining myself through my roles as a husband and father that I struggled to recognize who I was without those roles. It was a difficult season, one where I questioned everything, even my purpose. I needed something to help me rediscover who I was and why I mattered. That's when I turned to StrengthsFinder 2.0, which introduced me to the CliftonStrengths assessment.[1]

Originally known as StrengthsFinder, the tool has since been rebranded by Gallup as CliftonStrengths, in honor of its founder, psychologist Donald Clifton. But the core ideas remain the same: Every person has innate talents—unique strengths embedded deep in who they are—and true growth and fulfillment come not from fixing your weaknesses, but from understanding and leaning into what you naturally do best.

The book includes a code to take the online assessment, which quickly guides you through a series of timed questions designed to capture your instinctive preferences. The result is a list of your top five signature themes—things like Relator, Strategic, Learner, or Responsibility—which are not just traits but patterns of thinking, feeling, and behaving that show up when you're operating at your best.

For me, taking the assessment wasn't just informational, it was transformational. It gave me language for parts of myself I had lost touch with. It reminded me that I wasn't broken, that I was uniquely wired. It didn't answer every question I had about my future, but it reintroduced me to who I had always been.

The assessment identified "Communication" as my top strength, and when I read the description, it hit home. It explained that I had a gift for engaging people, drawing them into conversation, and helping them feel heard. Whether in group discussions or one-on-one conversations, I had an ability to bring out the best in others through dialogue. I naturally energized discussions and acknowledged the value in what others said, which encouraged even the quietest voices to speak up. This wasn't just something I liked doing, it was something God had designed me to do. My ability to foster open communication and create connections was a reflection of God's character at work in me.

But my assessment didn't stop with communication. My other top strengths—Strategic, Relator, Focus, and Futuristic—painted a fuller picture of who I was. I realized that my tendency to think ahead, plan, and see possibilities even in difficult situations were other ways I reflected God's foresight and wisdom.

One of the most surprising results was seeing "Relator" among my top strengths. At that time I was in the middle of a broken relationship, feeling like I had failed in one of the most important areas of my life—my marriage. I remember wondering how I could be good at relationships if I couldn't keep mine together. But CliftonStrengths reminded me that being a Relator wasn't about perfection, it was about my natural ability to build deep, meaningful connections with people.

The description of Relator emphasized my gift for forming authentic bonds, for valuing close relationships and being able to foster trust and open communication. This hit me in a profound way. It helped rebuild my confidence, reminding me that just because one relationship had ended didn't mean I was incapable of strong, healthy connections. In fact, the very strength I thought I had lost was actually a key part of who I was. Being a Relator wasn't just a skill; it was part of the unique way God had wired me. It reminded me that my uniqueness was not just a byproduct of my experiences; it was a part of God's intentional design.

For many people, discovering their strengths through tools like StrengthsFinder can be a pivotal moment. It's not about finding a label for yourself, it's about discovering how God has equipped you to contribute uniquely to the world. Whether your strength is in creativity, leadership, empathy, or problem-solving, these traits are divine fingerprints and evidence of the *imago Dei* in you. When I realized that, it changed my paradigm. I no longer saw my gifts as random quirks or isolated talents. I began to see my strengths as intentional reflections of God's character. And as I started leaning into those strengths, I saw how they could be used to help others. The more I reflected on them, the more I realized that the parts of myself I had once hidden or suppressed were meant to enrich the lives of those around me. My individuality was designed to be a blessing, not a burden, in my relationships.

WHY WE HIDE OUR LIGHT

This realization was a game-changer. We often enter relationships— whether romantic, familial, or professional—believing that compromise means erasing parts of ourselves to make others feel more comfortable. Think about the last time you were in a room full of people—maybe it was at work, a social event, or a family gathering. Can you remember that subtle, almost imperceptible shift you made in yourself just to blend in? Can you remember slightly adjusting your tone or softening your opinions so they wouldn't stand out too much? Have you ever stayed quiet when you had something to say, worried that your thoughts might ruffle feathers or make people uncomfortable? Or maybe it was as simple as nodding along in agreement with something you didn't truly believe just to avoid conflict.

It happens so easily, doesn't it? Without realizing it, we slip into this mode of accommodation, where we begin to edit ourselves— leaving out the parts we fear others might not like or, worse, might reject. We downplay our intelligence so we don't come off as "too much." We hide our creativity because it seems impractical to others. We don't share our ideas because we're afraid of being judged for thinking differently. The truth is, many of us have mastered the art of shrinking ourselves to fit the boxes others have built for us. We tell ourselves that it's easier this way, that blending in will keep the peace, that it's better to avoid standing out. Have you convinced yourself that people will like you more if you're less of yourself? Do you smooth over your perceived rough edges or dim your light?

At first it might feel like you're making things easier on yourself—less conflict, fewer uncomfortable moments. But over time you start to feel the weight of that shrinking. You begin to notice that you've carved away pieces of who you truly are. You're no longer fully yourself in your relationships, in your workplace, or even in your own home. It feels as though you're presenting a version of yourself, a curated and polished image, while the real you sits in the background, unseen and unexpressed.

The saddest part is, the more you hide yourself, the more disconnected you feel—not just from the people around you, but from yourself. You wonder why it's so hard to feel truly known by others, why there's a constant sense of emptiness in your interactions. You long for deeper connection, but you're terrified that being your full, authentic self might push people away.

Could it be, deep down, that you've come to believe that who you are isn't enough, that your quirks, your opinions, your dreams aren't worth sharing? Have you internalized the idea that you need to tone yourself down to be accepted? In doing so, have you hidden the very gifts God has placed within you, the very things God intentionally created? The irony is that while you're working so hard to fit in, you're robbing the world—and yourself—of the richness of your true identity.

This happens in relationships all the time. You enter a new relationship, and in the beginning, everything feels exciting. You want to make a good impression, so you downplay the parts of yourself you think might be too much for the other person to handle. Maybe you don't talk about your big dreams because they seem unrealistic or out of reach. Maybe you don't share your deepest thoughts, afraid that vulnerability might scare them away. Or perhaps you shift your personality just enough to match theirs so that everything feels smooth, like you're in sync. Many of us long for the feeling that we have lots in common with someone else.

But over time this takes its toll. You begin to feel trapped in the version of yourself that you've presented, knowing it doesn't reflect the fullness of who you are. You realize that the relationship is built on the foundation of a half-truth—not because you lied, but because you withheld the entirety of yourself. And now you're left wondering if the other person would love or accept you if they really knew you, or if they've only fallen in love with the version of you that fits neatly into their expectations.

In a professional setting this process might look different, but the feeling is the same. You sit in meetings, holding back your ideas because you worry they'll be too radical or different. You see others speaking up, offering their insights, and you wonder why you can't find the courage to do the same. But you've learned that in order to survive, whether it's climbing the corporate ladder or keeping your job, you need to fit in. You need to follow the unspoken rules, stay within the boundaries, and avoid making waves. So you stay in your lane even when you know deep down that you have something valuable to offer.

You tell yourself it's for the greater good, that it's easier this way, but inside you feel like you're withering. Your voice grows quieter. Your confidence fades. You wonder if you've lost the part of yourself that used to be bold, the part that wasn't afraid to stand out. It feels like the things that once made you come alive—your ideas, your creativity, your unique perspective—have been buried under layers of conformity.

This is the cost of downplaying ourselves. We sacrifice authenticity for acceptance, and in doing so, we cheat ourselves out of the fullness of life and relationships that God intended for us. The more we shrink, the more we distance ourselves from the *imago Dei*, the divine image within us. We were never meant to fit into someone else's mold. We were designed to stand out, to reflect God's character in the unique way he created us to do so.

GOD WANTS US TO SHINE

God didn't make us different just for the sake of variety. He designed each of us with qualities that, when brought into relationship with others, create something greater than the sum of their parts. Our distinctiveness allows us to bring unique perspectives, solutions, and strengths to the table, enriching the lives of those around us.

Think about it: Just as God is diverse in character—loving, just, creative, and wise—so too are we made to reflect these qualities in different ways. Some of us are naturally empathetic, while others are more strategic or visionary. Some of us thrive in environments where we can offer comfort and care, while others are most alive when solving complex problems or leading others with clarity. When we embrace these qualities, we offer something indispensable to the people we love. Our relationships are strengthened not in spite of our differences, but because of them.

I remember thinking about this in the context of my own relationships. For years I had believed that part of being in a relationship meant softening certain aspects of myself so I would be easier to love, to work with, or to be around. But what I came to understand was that the parts of myself I had tried to suppress were the very things that could bring depth and strength to my relationships, if only I had the courage to allow them to shine.

In marriage, for instance, we often face challenges because of differences in personality, perspective, or even pace. I had learned this firsthand in my own marriage. But instead of seeing these differences as obstacles, what if we viewed them as opportunities? What if, rather than trying to change our partner or ourselves, we leaned into the ways our uniqueness could complement one another?

The apostle Paul writes in 1 Corinthians about the body of Christ and how each member has a different role to play: "For the body is not one member, but many" (1 Corinthians 12:14). While Paul was speaking about spiritual gifts in the church, this could also be a powerful metaphor for how our differences work together to create something beautiful in our relationships. Each of us brings something unique to the table, and together we form a complete picture of God's creativity and design.

Embracing our individual distinctiveness means understanding that our strengths, passions, and even our struggles are part of the fabric of a relationship's strength. When we are fully ourselves, bringing our whole being to the relationship, we allow space for the other person to do the same. Authenticity breeds authenticity, and in that space, true connection is born.

I learned that in order to truly enrich my relationships, I had to embrace the very things that made me feel different. I had to stop trying to fit into a mold others expected and instead offer the gifts God had woven into my being. This shift, while not easy, was transformative. It allowed me to love more fully, to lead more boldly, and to connect more deeply. It allowed me to see that my distinctiveness was not a flaw to be corrected but a gift to be celebrated.

But this journey isn't just about accepting our own uniqueness. It's about extending that same grace to others. When we begin to see our own distinctiveness as a divine gift, it changes how we view the people around us. Instead of wishing they were more like us or trying to change them to fit our expectations, we begin to value the ways they are different. We begin to see their uniqueness as something that enriches the relationship, not something that needs to be fixed.

As I began to reclaim the parts of myself I once suppressed, something powerful clicked into place: I wasn't just uniquely made, I was intentionally made. And I wasn't alone in that truth. The same God who handcrafted my strengths and wiring did the same for every person I'd ever met or would meet in the future. If my uniqueness isn't a mistake, then neither is theirs. Our differences aren't problems to solve; they are pieces of a divine pattern that stretches all the way back to the beginning.

PONDER POINTS

1. What if the parts of yourself you've tried to hide are actually the most sacred reflections of how God designed you?

2. What if your quirks, your passions, your way of thinking—everything that makes you different—are not flaws to fix but gifts to offer?

Prayer

God, help me believe there's nothing wrong with who you created me to be. Quiet the lies that tell me I'm too much or not enough. Teach me to see myself as you see me—intentionally crafted, deeply loved, and divinely designed. Amen.

2

DESIGNED TO BE DIFFERENT

A Look at Creation

From the very first chapter of Genesis, God's commitment to diversity is on full display. The creation story is not just an account of how the world began, it's a reflection of God's love for variety, for uniqueness, for the beauty that emerges when different elements come together in harmony. At the heart of the biblical creation narrative is a profound message: Diversity was not an accident or afterthought, it was part of God's intentional design from the beginning.

When we read Genesis 1, we see a God who creates not just one thing but many things. He didn't create a single type of tree or flower but countless varieties—each distinct, each beautiful in its own way. He didn't make one kind of animal to roam the earth but a vast array of creatures, each perfectly suited to its environment. And when it came to humanity, God followed the same pattern. He didn't create us all the same. He made us each with different characteristics, talents, and personalities—each suited for our environment. God knew that our differences would be the source of strength, beauty, and balance.

When we examine the creation story, it's easy to overlook the profound depth and meaning behind God's words. Genesis isn't just a story about how life began, it's a blueprint for how God designed humanity, relationships, and the world itself. Every word holds significance, and within it lies the key to understanding our purpose, our authority, and the relationship dynamics God intended from the start.

KINGDOM AND DOMINION: A ROYAL EDICT FROM THE CREATOR

From the beginning, God entrusted humanity with responsibility. In Genesis 1:28 we read, "Be fruitful, and multiply, and replenish the earth, and subdue it: and have dominion over the fish of the sea, and over the fowl of the air, and over every living thing that moveth upon the earth."

This commissioning wasn't simply a beautiful line of poetry, it was a divine instruction to care for and cultivate the earth. The original Hebrew words—*kavash* (subdue) and *radah* (have dominion)—carry weight, but they're often misunderstood. Scholars remind us that this was not permission to dominate or exploit but a call to stewardship.[1] The earth and all its creatures were to be responsibly managed, nurtured, and protected. Creation care is not a modern environmental trend, it's a command rooted in the very first pages of Scripture.

While God gave this instruction to humanity as a whole, I've come to understand and apply this passage in a deeply personal way. When I read Genesis 1:28, I see more than a global mandate— I see an invitation. Not only are we called to care for the earth, but I believe each of us has been entrusted with a unique sphere of influence, a space in which our gifts, passions, and wisdom are meant to flourish and bless others.

You might call it your assignment, your calling, or your lane. I think of it as a personal domain—a place in life where you've been uniquely positioned to create, lead, nurture, or serve. That domain might be your family, your profession, your art, your neighborhood, or even a message you're called to carry. And while this isn't explicitly stated in the Genesis text, it's an application that has helped me live with clarity and intentionality.

What's important is this: God created each of us with something to cultivate. Just as Adam and Eve were placed in the garden to tend and keep it, we've each been given spaces, literal or metaphorical, to steward. And when we understand that, we begin to live differently. We begin to lead with care, create with purpose, and serve with love.

Too often we forget that we're part of something sacred. We lose sight of the fact that we were made not just to exist but to participate. When we remember that we've been entrusted by God with influence, resources, and relationships, it becomes easier to live with intention. We're not owners but stewards. Not rulers but caretakers.

MALE AND FEMALE: A SHARED REFLECTION OF GOD'S IMAGE

Before we begin to explore how men and women navigate differences in relationships, we need to return to the beginning—the creation stories in Genesis. And yes, there are two of them. Genesis 1 and Genesis 2 are widely considered by scholars to reflect two distinct traditions: one emphasizing humanity's shared vocation as image bearers of God (Genesis 1) and the other focusing more personally on the relationship between the man and the woman (Genesis 2).[2]

In Genesis 1:26-27 we read, "And God said, Let us make man in our image, after our likeness. . . . So God created man in his own image, in the image of God created he him; male and female created he them." This passage offers no hint of hierarchy, only shared dignity and divine reflection. Both male and female are made in God's image. Both are blessed. Both are commissioned to be fruitful, multiply, and steward the earth. The emphasis here is on unity in vocation and equality in worth.

Genesis 2, however, zooms in. It offers a more intimate and narrative account of human creation and introduces a second character, formed not from the dust this time but from the side of the first human. This has led some to assume gender hierarchy. But a closer look at the Hebrew text complicates that reading in beautiful ways.

The Hebrew word *adam*, used in the early verses of Genesis 2, simply means "human" or "earthling." It is not a male proper name, nor is it inherently gendered.[3] Only later, in Genesis 2:23, when the second human is fashioned, do the terms *iysh* (man) and *iyshah* (woman) appear—both drawn from the same linguistic root, symbolizing shared origin and connection.

What Genesis 2 paints is not a story of one being split into two, nor a case of one superior and one subordinate. Rather, it's a depiction of mutuality—a picture of two persons created for relational interdependence, not competition, hierarchy, or control.

What Does "Helper" Really Mean?
Exploring *Ezer Kenegdo*

One phrase in Genesis 2 has been the subject of countless sermons, books, and unfortunately, misconceptions: *ezer kenegdo*. When the first human is found to be "not good" alone, God declares the intent to make a "help meet for him" (Genesis 2:18). The Hebrew phrase is *ezer kenegdo*, often translated "helper fit for him." But this English rendering flattens its depth.

The word *ezer* appears twenty-one times in the Old Testament. In the majority of those cases, it refers to God as Israel's help—a powerful, life-saving presence. Psalm 121:2, for example, says, "My help cometh from the LORD, which made heaven and earth." Clearly, this is not the kind of help that fits most antiquated gender stereotypes about a woman's role in relationships.

So when *ezer* is applied to the woman in Genesis 2, it cannot mean assistant or subordinate. It speaks of someone who brings essential strength, presence, and assistance in mission, not unlike how God helps his people.

The second word, *kenegdo*, literally means "corresponding to" or "alongside," indicating one who stands face-to-face, not behind or beneath.[4] Together, *ezer kenegdo* suggests a counterpart who is equal in value, different in perspective, and essential in partnership.

It's important not to overinterpret this phrase as proof of a specific theology of gender roles. It's one phrase in one chapter of one tradition. And yet it powerfully affirms that neither man nor woman was created to be less-than, or even the same as, but was uniquely equipped to live and work alongside the other in shared purpose and calling.

THE POWER OF PARTNERSHIP

Sadly, the phrase *ezer kenegdo* has often been misunderstood or watered down. In some church traditions, it's been interpreted to mean women were created to support from the sidelines, to follow rather than lead. The result has been a subtle (and sometimes not-so-subtle) message that women are somehow less essential in God's mission.

But that's not the picture Genesis gives us.

The woman is created as a corresponding partner, not to follow from behind but to stand face-to-face. Not to be quiet and compliant but to contribute fully. Not to be a complement but to be a colaborer. And this mutuality isn't just theological. It's practical, personal, and deeply relational.

Women have often carried unseen loads—managing homes, nurturing communities, noticing emotional shifts long before they're spoken aloud. These aren't just personality traits; they're strengths. When seen through the lens of *ezer kenegdo*, these strengths aren't secondary, they're sacred.

I've spoken to countless women who've felt like they had to shrink their voices to make space for someone else's insecurities. Others have been told that their leadership must look a certain way—or not at all.

Genesis 2 invites us to see not just that we are different, but that our differences are designed for interdependence. The woman is not described as a clone nor as a subordinate. She is presented as someone who can stand opposite—*kenegdo*—and offer what the other does not have. This is not about dividing the world into pink and blue tasks. It's about acknowledging that none of us was created to do life alone. The human condition isn't just about self-expression, it's about connection. And connection works best when we stop assuming sameness and start appreciating how someone else's way of thinking, feeling, or approaching the world might fill in what we lack.

EMBRACING OUR DIFFERENCES AS SACRED DESIGN

The diversity between man and woman is not a mistake. It is part of the beauty of God's creation. Genesis 1:27 says, "So God created man in his own image, in the image of God created he him; male and female created he them."

From the very beginning, God chose to reflect his image through both male and female. Not through sameness, but through difference. This doesn't just apply to gender, it applies to all of us. Our personalities, backgrounds, talents, and ways of thinking are part of a bigger picture. When we embrace that diversity, in ourselves and others, we begin to experience the richness of what God intended for human relationships.

That's why this book isn't about erasing differences. It's about learning how to hold them well. When we stop trying to mold people into our image, and instead honor the image of God in them, something powerful happens: We grow. Our relationships deepen. And we begin to see conflict not as something to avoid, but as a doorway to greater connection.

Let's be honest: The way we've often talked about gender, especially in faith spaces, has left a lot of people carrying quiet questions. Questions like: Do I matter in the same way? Does my perspective count? Is there space for me to lead, to speak, to be fully myself without being asked to tone it down?

If you've asked those questions, you're not alone.

If we're willing to slow down and really listen, what Genesis shows us is that from the very beginning, both man and woman were created with dignity, agency, and purpose. The woman isn't brought in to assist a mission that's already underway. She's formed to share in the work of cultivating, protecting, and reflecting the image of God in the world.

That means her presence isn't supplemental. It's essential.

And not because of what she can do, or how well she carries invisible loads, or how many roles she balances. Her value doesn't come from performance—it comes from identity. She was created in God's image, full stop. And so was he. The difference between them isn't a matter of status, it's a reflection of God's creativity.

The truth is, all of us—regardless of gender—have moments where we question if we belong, if our wiring is too different, if our voice will be heard. And Genesis 1 responds with a quiet but unwavering truth: Yes. You belong. As you are. With purpose.

UNDERSTANDING DIVERSITY

When we think about diversity, we often think of physical differences—race, gender, and culture. But diversity is so much more than that. It's diversity in thought, in perspective, in experience, in talent. God's creation reflects this. Imagine a world where every person was the same: thought the same, acted the same, and had the same abilities. It would be a world devoid of color, of innovation, of growth. Diversity is not just something to be accepted, it's something to be celebrated, because it is a reflection of the Creator's brilliance.

Consider the earth itself. God could have chosen to create a single type of landscape, but instead God filled the world with mountains, oceans, forests, and deserts. Each landscape, unique and distinct, plays a role in the ecosystem. Each environment supports life in a different way, contributing to the overall balance of the world. In the same way, God designed humanity to be diverse, each of us playing a unique role in the grand design. We are not meant to be the same. Our differences are what make the world beautiful and what allow us to function together as one body.

The diversity we see in creation serves as a powerful metaphor for human relationships. Just as the earth thrives because of its varied landscapes, our relationships thrive when we embrace the diversity within them. We weren't meant to have relationships only with people who are exactly like us. In fact, the richness of any relationship—whether it's a marriage, friendship, or professional partnership—comes from the differences we bring to the table. Just as no two landscapes are exactly the same, no two people are exactly the same. And that's the beauty of it.

Despite this clear design for diversity, we often resist it. In our relationships we tend to gravitate toward those who we believe think like us, act like us, and share our perspectives. We find comfort in sameness because it's familiar. But God's design for diversity invites us to step outside of that comfort zone. It calls us to embrace those who are different, to seek out relationships that challenge us and help us grow. Just as the different elements of creation come together to form a beautiful, balanced world, so do our relationships flourish when we embrace diversity.

Think back to the creation of Adam and Eve. God didn't make Eve a carbon copy of Adam. He created her to be different. Their relationship wasn't meant to be one of uniformity but of partnership—two different people, reflecting different aspects of God's image, coming together to form a stronger whole. This is the essence of God's design for relationships: unity through diversity. It's not about erasing our differences, but about learning how our differences can enhance and strengthen each other. This book provides you with tools. Tools you will need to navigate, embrace, and celebrate your "irreconcilable" differences.

Differences are woven into the fabric of creation, and they are also woven into the fabric of human relationships. When we resist our differences, we resist God's design. We reject the very things that make relationships dynamic and full of potential. But when we embrace our differences, when we lean into the discomfort of diversity, we open ourselves up to a fuller, richer experience of life and love. We allow God to work through our differences, revealing his character in ways that we could never experience if we all stayed the same.

So what does this mean for you? It means that the very things that make you different, the qualities that set you apart from others, are not flaws. They are not accidents. They are not weaknesses. They are not to be hidden. They are intentional parts of God's design for your life. The differences you bring into your relationships, your workplace, and your community are gifts. And just as important, the differences others bring are gifts as well. When we stop trying to mold ourselves and others into something we are not (and they are not), we make space for God's creativity to flourish in our lives.

Diversity is an invitation. An invitation to step into relationships with a new perspective—one that values differences, that seeks out uniqueness, and that understands the beauty of a world where no two people are the same. It's an invitation to see diversity not as something to overcome but as something to embrace, something to celebrate. When we do this, we honor God's design and we experience the fullness of what it means to live in relationship with others.

Difference is not something to fear, fix, or flatten. It's something to honor. Whether we're talking about gender, personality, gifts, or roles, what makes us unique is also what makes us essential. The Genesis story—read carefully and in context—doesn't pit man against woman or call one to follow while the other leads. It shows us a God who delights in distinction, who creates with intention, and who invites us into partnership, not just with him, but with one another. When we recognize our shared image-bearing identity and learn to value the distinct ways we each reflect God's nature, we move from tolerating difference to thriving within it. And that shift changes everything.

PONDER POINTS

1. What if your differences, and the differences of others, aren't roadblocks to avoid, but revelations of God's creativity?

2. What if learning to embrace what makes us unique is one of the most spiritual things we can do in a relationship?

PRAYER

God, thank you for designing me and others with intentional differences. Help me to celebrate the beauty of diversity, not just in the world around me but in the relationships I hold most dear. Teach me to see every difference not as a threat, but as an invitation to love more deeply, listen more carefully, and reflect your image more clearly. Amen.

3

EMBRACING THE PEOPLE WHO DRIVE YOU CRAZY

Have you ever found yourself asking, "Why can't they just think like I do?" Whether it's a spouse, coworker, child, or friend, we all encounter people whose way of operating feels frustrating, even foreign. Maybe you thrive on structure and they live in chaos. Or maybe you love open-ended brainstorming while they want a concrete plan. Whatever the contrast, these relational frictions can leave us questioning compatibility, communication, and even calling.

But what if the very differences that annoy us most were never meant to be problems to fix? What if they were pieces of God's design to embrace?

When God created us, he did so with intention. Every aspect of who we are—our personality, our gifts, our strengths, and even our weaknesses—was crafted with a specific purpose in mind. And while this purpose is personal, it is also relational. Our differences not only serve to complement one another but also reflect the unique domains we are called to influence in the world.

Think about it: Why are we all so different? Why is it that some people are naturally drawn to think more creatively while others (who might also think creatively) lean more heavily on process and structure? Why do some excel in the spotlight, while others feel more at home behind the scenes? The answer lies in the fact that each of us is created to fulfill a unique role, to exercise dominion over a specific domain. Our differences are not arbitrary; they are tailored to the specific calling and territory God has entrusted to us.

CALLED TO DIFFERENT DOMAINS: DISCOVERING YOUR UNIQUE PATH TO IMPACT

God created us with differences so we might influence different areas of life, what we might call "domains of purpose" or "calling." In Genesis 1:28, when God blessed humanity and said, "Be fruitful, and multiply, and replenish the earth, and subdue it," the charge was given not to an individual but to humankind as a whole. As we've already explored, this dominion wasn't about domination, it was a divine commission to steward creation with care, intention, and responsibility.[1] And while the command is shared, the expression of that calling plays out uniquely in each life.

Not everyone is wired to carry out their stewardship in the same way. Some people are drawn toward environments that prioritize beauty, imagination, and expressive potential—places where meaning is shaped through art, language, or emotion. Others are energized by systems, strategy, and logistic complexity, where order, structure, and problem-solving take center stage. But it's important to recognize that these domains aren't opposites. They are overlapping, complementary dimensions of the same human calling.

Even those in artistic or innovative spaces rely on structure, discipline, and logic to bring their visions to life. Likewise, those who build systems or lead in highly analytical spaces benefit from creative thinking, emotional intelligence, and intuition. The distinction is not about who uses structure versus who doesn't, but about where each person begins, the primary strategies they lean on to move through the world and make meaning of their purpose.

A filmmaker and a financial planner may both operate with precision and creativity, but the way those strengths show up, and the problems they are designed to solve, differ. One brings stories to life that shape culture and awaken empathy. The other brings clarity to uncertainty, helping people build toward secure and flourishing futures. Both are fulfilling the Genesis mandate. Both are stewarding what they've been entrusted with. And both are necessary for a world that thrives.

God's design is not for everyone to fit into the same mold but to recognize the mold they've been given and to form it faithfully. Diversity in this sense is not just a social virtue, it is a sacred strategy embedded in the blueprint of creation.

A person who is called to the arts will need different tools than someone called to engineering or finance. Just as a gardener needs different tools than a builder, we need different qualities, skills, and ways of thinking to thrive in our respective areas. These differences aren't flaws, they are functional. They are what make us uniquely suited to our particular image of God.

But what happens when only one perspective, one voice, or one way of thinking dominates? Let's look at the role of pastors and leaders within a church or organization. Imagine a pastor who speaks forty to fifty-two weeks out of the year to their congregation. While that one pastor may be gifted, wise, and full of insight, the lack of diverse voices can lead to a spiritual, emotional, and intellectual emptiness for many members of the congregation. No one person can meet the spiritual and emotional needs of an entire community, and relying on a single perspective limits the congregation's ability to experience the full breadth of God's wisdom.

Each person in a congregation comes from a different background, has different experiences, and brings a unique set of spiritual needs to the table. It is impossible for one leader to fully connect with everyone, no matter how gifted they are. That's why it's crucial for churches to bring in multiple voices, perspectives, and leaders who can speak to the hearts of different people. When a church allows for various thought leaders to share the pulpit, it creates space for the entire congregation to be fed, nurtured, and challenged in different ways.

Diversity of thought in leadership isn't just about variety, it's about depth. One person's leadership may inspire creativity and vision, while another may bring practical wisdom and structure. When pastors and leaders collaborate and share the platform, the congregation has a fuller, richer spiritual experience. Think of it this way: just as we are called to different domains in life, different pastors or leaders are called to different aspects of teaching and shepherding. One leader may focus on spiritual healing, another on social justice, and yet another on biblical doctrine. When all of these voices come together, the congregation is strengthened in ways one person alone could never achieve.

When churches lack this diversity of thought, their congregations may feel spiritually empty or disconnected. Why? Because not everyone can relate to the same message or the same speaker week after week. When leadership lacks diversity, it unintentionally leaves certain groups feeling unheard, misunderstood, or disconnected from the larger mission. And just as in any relationship where differences are ignored or suppressed, growth becomes stagnant.

Pastors and leaders need to embrace this diversity not only to reach different members of the congregation but to reflect the diversity in the body of Christ. Paul, in 1 Corinthians 12:12, emphasizes the importance of different parts of the body working together, each with a unique function: "For as the body is one, and hath many members, and all the members of that one body, being many, are one body: so also is Christ." A church that allows multiple leaders to speak tends to (though not always) reflect the diversity of the body of Christ, where different gifts, perspectives, and strengths come together to build a stronger, more unified whole.

Just as no two individuals are alike, no two leaders are called to lead in the same way. An organization, like any relationship, flourishes when its leaders embrace their differences and work together to create a richer, more complete experience for everyone. Diversity of thought, when embraced in leadership, mirrors a more intentional design for relationships—each person or leader brings something unique that enhances the whole.

It's important to acknowledge that differences in relationships aren't always easy. In fact, they often create friction, frustration, and misunderstanding. If you've ever been in a relationship—whether in marriage, a close friendship, or a working partnership—with someone whose strengths are vastly different from yours, you know how difficult it can be. It might feel like you're speaking two completely different languages, constantly misinterpreting each other or getting stuck on the same issues. But here's the thing: this friction isn't without purpose.

The Bible tells us, "Iron sharpeneth iron; so a man sharpeneth the countenance of his friend" (Proverbs 27:17). And just as iron can't be sharpened without some form of friction, our differences often challenge us in ways that lead to growth. These challenges push us out of our comfort zones, forcing us to see things from a different perspective, to stretch beyond what we think we know, and to learn new ways of thinking and being.

Imagine this: You're someone who thrives on spontaneity and creativity. You love the excitement of doing things on the fly—making plans at the last minute, trying new ideas without a rigid schedule. Maybe you feel most alive when you're following your passion in the moment. Now imagine being in a relationship with someone who craves structure, routine, and predictability. This person finds peace in knowing exactly what the day will hold, planning things well in advance, and sticking to a clear schedule. You can already picture the tension this dynamic creates, can't you?

One person feels stifled by too much planning, while the other feels unsettled by too much spontaneity. Every time you suggest something spontaneous, your partner might react with resistance or even anxiety. Likewise, when they insist on planning everything down to the minute, you might feel frustrated and confined. At first, it seems like these differences are barriers that keep you from connecting on a deeper level. But here's the truth: those differences are actually what can bring you together in a more meaningful way if you choose to see them as opportunities, not obstacles. Maybe your spontaneous energy brings excitement and creativity to your partner's life, helping them loosen up and see the beauty of being flexible. And in turn, their structure and routine could help bring balance and more stability to your life, grounding your creative ideas and helping you follow through on projects that might otherwise remain unfinished. Together you learn to blend your strengths, creating a partnership that is not only more balanced but also more fulfilling.

I once coached a couple we'll call John and Sarah. I remember when John and Sarah's marriage came to a crossroad. John, a numbers guy, worked in finance and approached life the way he approached spreadsheets: logical, methodical, and precise. John might describe himself as somewhat spontaneous, but it certainly was not his primary strength. Every day was mapped out with meticulous care, from morning routines to evening plans. He had a habit of creating schedules down to the minute—even their weekend grocery trips had a set time limit and route. His day planner was one of his most valued possessions, a symbol of control and predictability in a world that felt chaotic to him. He found comfort in knowing exactly what was happening and when.

Sarah was the opposite in almost every way. She preferred spontaneity whenever she could find it. The walls of their home were lined with her vibrant paintings, a reflection of her free-spirited soul. Her life was a swirl of color, emotion, and intuition, and she loved to go with the flow, letting the day unfold organically. While she didn't hate structure—in fact, her days were well-organized—when it came to her relationship and her time to relate to John, structure made her feel suffocated, like her creativity was being caged. She wanted the freedom to decide at the last minute that they were taking a road trip or that dinner plans would be whatever inspired her in the moment. For Sarah, life was about living in the present, experiencing beauty and joy as they appeared, unplanned. Sarah spent her workdays in a structured and rigid context, so in her relationship she craved spontaneity.

In the early years of their marriage, this difference—what seemed at first like a cute contrast—slowly became a source of tension. John would feel anxious when Sarah didn't stick to a plan or when her spontaneous ideas disrupted his perfectly scheduled day. For instance, they would agree on a quiet evening at home, but Sarah might decide at the last minute that they should drive out to the beach to catch the sunset or go visit friends. John, feeling blindsided, would dig in his heels, unable to enjoy the moment because it was not part of the plan. He saw her spontaneity as irresponsible, a chaotic element that threw his orderly life into disarray.

Meanwhile, Sarah felt smothered by John's incessant need to plan. She would wake up excited about the possibility of a day full of discovery, only to have her joy deflated by John's rigid timetable. "How can you plan creativity?" she would ask in frustration. The more John tried to enforce structure, the more she resisted, often opting to pursue her own plans even if it caused friction. She began to wonder if they were truly compatible, feeling like her need for creativity was being stifled under the weight of John's schedules.

Their home, once filled with laughter and love, started to feel like a battlefield, where every conversation turned into a negotiation about time, plans, and control. John would argue for the necessity of predictability: "How do you expect us to get things done if we don't plan for it?" Sarah would counter with, "When have I ever not gotten things done?" And, "How do you expect to enjoy life if you're constantly trying to control everything?"

Eventually, they both wondered if their relationship had run its course. They loved each other deeply, but their differences felt like an unbridgeable chasm. They were speaking different languages— they wanted closeness and connection but were going about it in two different ways.

Instead of giving up, they chose to lean into their differences. After one particularly heated argument, they decided to seek help, hoping they could find a way to reconnect without losing themselves in the process. In our sessions we explored their frustrations, but more importantly, we began to shift their perspective on those very differences that were causing them pain.

Over time, John began to realize that Sarah's spontaneity wasn't chaos, it was creativity in its purest form. Her ability to see the beauty in the moment, to go off script and embrace life as it unfolded, was actually an asset he had overlooked in his own life. He began to see how Sarah's free spirit brought life, color, and joy into their home in a way his spreadsheets never could. But something else came out of the sessions that neither of us saw coming. John realized that he had stereotyped Sarah. Subconsciously he felt that her need for spontaneity in their relationship stemmed from irresponsibility. It meant she lacked the order needed to get things done. What he did not account for was how successful Sarah was in other areas of life that did not include him. She had risen to the top of her field, and that does not happen without order and discipline. When Sarah was done with her day at the office, she preferred to lean into her spontaneous side. She wanted to enjoy her evenings and weekends with John like they had when they'd first met.

John, on the other hand, was living one-dimensionally. Everything was one way, and because of it, life seemed monotonous. In one of our sessions, John admitted that he was depressed but still functioning at a high level. That admission opened all of our eyes.

Slowly, John started to relax his grip on his rigid schedules, giving himself permission to be flexible. One Saturday morning, instead of mapping out their day in advance, John let go and decided to enjoy the moment. He and Sarah ended up spending the day wandering the city, discovering art galleries, cafés, and street performers—an adventure he would never have planned but thoroughly enjoyed. He realized that letting go didn't mean chaos; it meant gaining a new kind of freedom.

For Sarah, the change in perspective was equally profound. She realized that John's structure wasn't about control for the sake of control, it was about security. His planning allowed their life to run smoothly, ensuring that bills were paid, meals were prepared, and their future was secure. Sarah began to appreciate that within the boundaries of John's structure, she had the space and stability to create freely. His planning gave her the freedom to dive deeper into her art without worrying about the details of everyday life. She started to see his schedules not as limitations but as a framework that supported their life together.

A major turning point came during a family vacation. Sarah had always dreaded these trips because they were usually planned down to the hour, leaving little room for spontaneous exploration. But this time they decided they would take one full day where there was no plan, no schedule. They spent that day wandering through a local market, discovering hidden trails, and stumbling upon a beautiful overlook where they watched the sunset. That night John admitted that it was one of the best days he'd had in years. Sarah, in turn, told him that she saw how his planning of the rest of the trip allowed them to enjoy their time without stress. She actually liked that he planned ahead because it took the burden off her. At work she was responsible for much of the planning, so at home she preferred not to have that responsibility.

Together they started to realize that their differences weren't obstacles but opportunities for growth. John learned to appreciate Sarah's spontaneity as a source of joy and inspiration, while Sarah came to see John's structure as a gift that freed her. Over time they stopped trying to change each other and began to embrace the ways their differences made their marriage stronger. What once felt like friction became the thing that refined them, making them a better version of themselves and a more united couple. They also started to incorporate each other's strengths into their own lives. Sarah began planning more while John started letting go, and as a result they reported having much more fun together.

WHAT IF IT'S NOT WHAT YOU THINK?

It's easy to form conclusions about people, especially when their behavior frustrates us. We assume they're trying to be difficult. We label them as selfish, lazy, rigid, or controlling. But what if those behaviors aren't the full story? What if what you're seeing on the surface is a response to something buried deeper—an old wound, a hidden fear, a story you've never heard? I would invite you to pause before you judge, to lean in before you label, and to consider that what you're reacting to might not be rebellion, it might be protection. Sometimes the very thing that drives us crazy about someone else is really just their way of surviving.

Imagine you're a parent who values discipline, order, and structure. You've worked hard to create a household where everything runs like clockwork—chores are done on time, homework is completed without a fight, and dinner is served promptly at six p.m. To you, this rhythm isn't about control, it's about love. It's how you create stability, express care, and protect your family from chaos.

Now picture your child: brilliant, imaginative, and completely uninterested in your systems. From a young age they've marched to the beat of their own drum. While you were organizing bedtime routines, they were inventing stories about talking animals. While you were laying out tomorrow's to-do list, they were building forts in the living room with no intention of cleaning up afterward.

They aren't defiant. They're just wired for wonder. But over time, their refusal to embrace the structure you've so carefully built starts to wear on you.

You've created a world that works. And they seem to be resisting it at every turn.

For example, let's say it's a school night and they have homework. You've carved out a quiet space, minimized distractions, and set a clear time for focus. But instead of opening their textbook, they're doodling dragons in the margins of a notebook. You remind them that time is ticking, and they nod, promising they'll start soon. But the minutes slip away. You're getting anxious. They're still sketching.

It's tempting in moments like these to assume laziness or disrespect. You might feel the need to clamp down—raise your voice, enforce a consequence, double down on the schedule. After all, structure works for you. But what if your child isn't trying to reject your love or sabotage the routine? What if their brain just works differently?

Not every child who resists structure has a diagnosis or disorder. Some are simply wired with a high need for imaginative freedom. They're not trying to challenge you, they're trying to find oxygen for their ideas. And the more they feel misunderstood, the more they retreat. Not out of rebellion but out of self-preservation.

This is where parenting becomes more than management—it becomes ministry. What if instead of viewing your child's behavior as a problem to correct, you see it as a window into their soul? What if beneath the frustration, you find a uniquely gifted mind waiting to be nurtured in a different way?

Imagine creating a rhythm that works for both of you. Perhaps it means giving them fifteen minutes of drawing before easing into homework. Or allowing them to pace while they read aloud. Or integrating their creativity into assignments, like illustrating a history lesson instead of just memorizing dates. Small adaptations, rooted in empathy, can open doors to deeper connection.

This isn't about lowering expectations—it's about expanding your understanding. It's about recognizing that love doesn't always look like order and routine, and brilliance doesn't always look like compliance. Your child may not be difficult—they may be different. And different doesn't mean disobedient. It means you've been given the sacred task of stewarding a soul that won't fit into someone else's mold. And maybe that's exactly how God intended it.

Take the story of a friend I once knew. Her daughter was an incredibly bright but free-spirited child, always more interested in making up stories and creating imaginary worlds than following the family's daily routine. The daughter's lack of attention to structure often frustrated her mom, who prided herself on organization. The tension between them grew as the daughter entered her teenage years, and there were countless arguments about responsibilities, curfews, and chores. At one point, the mother described her daughter as "impossible," lamenting that they seemed to be growing further apart by the day. (We'll talk about labeling shortly and why this is something you should stay away from in any relationship).

But something shifted one evening when the mother attended one of her daughter's art shows at school. As she walked through the gallery, she realized just how much her daughter's creativity had flourished over the years, despite their constant battles. That night she saw her daughter through new eyes—not as a rebellious teen, but as someone who saw the world in a way that was entirely different from her own view. The mother began to approach their relationship differently. Instead of trying to force her daughter into routines, she gave her more freedom to express herself and worked on finding balance. In turn, her daughter started to respect the boundaries and structures that had always been in place, because she no longer felt smothered by them.

This shift didn't happen overnight, but over time their relationship grew stronger. By embracing their differences, both mother and daughter learned to value what the other brought to the table. The mother began to see that her daughter's creativity and independence were reflections of her unique gifts. And the daughter, having been met with understanding, became more open to the structures her mother set, realizing they weren't meant to restrict her but to help her thrive.

PONDER POINTS

1. What if the person who frustrates you most isn't broken, but beautifully different?

2. What if their approach to life isn't a flaw, but a mirror inviting you to grow in areas you've ignored?

3. What if embracing their uniqueness could unlock a deeper strength in both of you?

PRAYER

God, give me eyes to see beyond the friction. Help me recognize the beauty in the differences you've placed in the people around me. Teach me not to react out of frustration but to respond with curiosity, compassion, and grace. Show me how to celebrate the gifts that others bring, even when they don't look like mine. May our differences not divide us, but shape us into something stronger—together. Amen.

4

WHEN BEHAVIOR IS
REALLY BIOGRAPHY

WE TEND TO JUDGE PEOPLE by what they do. She's so rigid.
He's always angry. They never show up on time. But what if those
behaviors aren't just quirks or character flaws? What if they're
stories written long before you entered the picture, shaped by
childhood wounds, survival instincts, or formative experiences
that left an imprint on how one sees the world?

According to Dr. Dan Siegel, renowned psychiatrist and
author of *The Whole-Brain Child*, behavior is often the "down-
stream expression" of unresolved emotion and unspoken
memory, especially in relationships, where past patterns are
unconsciously reenacted.[1] In other words, what looks like defiance or control on the surface may actually be a person's way
of coping with fear, instability, or emotional pain they've never
been able to name.

According to attachment theory, developed by psychologist
John Bowlby, the way we behave in adult relationships is significantly shaped by the caregiving environments of our early years.
These relational blueprints—formed through experiences of safety,
abandonment, nurture, or neglect—become the filters through
which we interpret others' actions and regulate our own.[2] What

we call "difficult" behavior might actually be someone's biography of trying to feel safe again.

Behavior, more often than not, is biography in motion. It's the external expression of internal history. And when we start to see people not just for what they do but what they've lived through, everything begins to change. Judgment softens. Compassion rises. And relationships that once felt impossible suddenly make more sense—not because the other person changed, but because our lens did.

Let's go back to John and Sarah for a moment. As Sarah's frustration with John's need for structure grew, so did the way she talked about it to others. "He's so controlling," she would say to her friends, rolling her eyes when they'd ask about their latest disagreement. The word "controlling" started to come up more and more in her conversations with family, too. "It's like he has to plan every minute of our lives," she'd say, feeling justified in venting her frustrations. The label stuck quickly—John became the "controlling" husband in the eyes of their family and friends. And who could blame her? To Sarah, John's need for order felt stifling, like a cage around her creativity. It wasn't just about the schedules; it was about the sense that she had no freedom to be herself outside of work, no space to explore or be spontaneous. When she said, "How do you expect to enjoy life if you're constantly trying to control everything?" it wasn't just a question, it was a cry for the life she felt she was missing. She saw John's need for structure as an attempt to dominate their life, and it was easy for her to label it as control.

But here's the problem with labels: They oversimplify complex realities. They reduce people to one-dimensional caricatures, ignoring the deeper motivations that drive their behavior. What Sarah didn't see, at least not at first, was that John's desire for structure was not about controlling her or dictating their life. It was about security. For John, planning and structure were his way of ensuring that everything would run smoothly, that their life together would be stable, and that they wouldn't face the chaos or uncertainty that deeply unsettled him.

The truth was, John was trying to protect their life together in the only way he knew how. But because Sarah didn't understand this deeper motivation, she misinterpreted his actions. The label "controlling" took root, and once it did, it started to color everything. The more she called him "controlling," the more John began to feel like the problem, even though his intentions were coming from a place of care.

This kind of labeling isn't unique to Sarah and John's story. It happens in many relationships. We see someone's behavior, and instead of understanding the deeper motivations behind it, we attach a label—controlling, lazy, selfish, demanding—and that label begins to define how we see them. We forget that people's behaviors are often driven by fears, insecurities, or desires that may not be immediately obvious. And once the label sticks, it becomes almost impossible to see past it.

Sarah, like many of us, fell into this trap. She started to view John only through the lens of control, and it began to erode her respect for him. Every time he suggested a plan or asked to stick to the schedule, it confirmed the label she had already assigned. She didn't see the careful thought or the love behind his actions; she only saw the restrictions it placed on her. Over time, this labeling created more distance between them, as Sarah felt increasingly suffocated and John felt increasingly misunderstood.

During one of our sessions, Sarah finally understood the "why" behind John's behavior, and when she did, everything shifted. We had been discussing why John was so attached to what seemed to her like overplanning, and he revealed something he had never fully explained to her. John shared that growing up, his family life had been chaotic, with financial instability, unpredictable parents, and constant uncertainty.

John talked about it like it was yesterday; he was eight years old, standing in the kitchen of their small apartment. The floor was peeling at the edges, the cupboards were nearly bare except for a few cans of soup, and the dim light above the table flickered as if it, too, was barely holding on. His parents were arguing about money, again. Money was always the problem. He could hear his father's voice rise, sharp and biting, as he blamed his mother for the missed rent payment, and his mother's voice breaking as she tried to defend herself, to explain how the bills had piled up despite her best efforts.

John sat at the edge of the kitchen table, watching the scene unfold. He wasn't part of the conversation—back then children weren't allowed to speak during the arguments—but he felt every word like a punch to his gut. There had been many nights like this, when the uncertainty of his family's future hung in the air like a storm cloud. But this night was different.

His mother, overwhelmed by the weight of their circumstances, finally broke down. "I don't know what we're going to do," she whispered through tears, her shoulders slumped in defeat. "We don't have enough to cover rent next month. We don't even have enough for groceries this week."

The room fell silent for a moment, and to John, the silence was deafening. He felt the weight of his mother's words settle over him like a heavy blanket, suffocating. There was no plan. There was no solution. Everything felt like it was spiraling out of control.

That's when his father slammed his hand on the table. The sound reverberated through the small apartment, making John flinch. "You can't even keep this family together!" his father yelled, his voice filled with anger and frustration. "We're always one step away from falling apart!"

The words hit John harder than any argument he'd heard before. He looked at his mother, defeated, with tears running down her cheeks, and something shifted inside him. His young mind couldn't articulate it, but in that moment, John subconsciously decided, *When I have my own family, this will never happen. I'll never let them live in this kind of chaos.*

For the first time John understood the fragility of life, how quickly things could unravel when there wasn't a plan, when nothing was predictable. The apartment, already small and cramped, felt like it was closing in on him. He could feel his heart pounding in his chest, and his stomach churned with the uncertainty that filled the room. He wanted to run, to escape the fear that was deeply lodged inside him. But more than that, he wanted to control the situation, to restore a sense of order and predictability.

That night John couldn't sleep. He lay in bed, staring at the ceiling, his parents' argument still echoing in his mind. He wondered if they would have to move again. Would his father leave? Would they be able to afford food next week? His young heart couldn't bear the weight of not knowing, of living in a world where everything felt so unstable.

From that night on, John became hyper-aware of the importance of control, of structure, of having a plan. He started noticing everything that was out of order in their life. The bills that piled up on the counter, the unanswered phone calls from what he assumed were creditors, the refrigerator that was never fully stocked. He noticed how his mother's face would grow more anxious every time the rent was due, how his father's temper would flare when something didn't go as expected. To John, unpredictability became the enemy—one he vowed to keep at bay, no matter what.

Even as a child, John began creating routines for himself. He would lay his clothes out the night before school, making sure everything was neatly folded and ready to go. He would organize his school supplies and pack his lunch with precision, double-checking that he had everything he needed. In a life that felt so wildly out of control, these small routines gave him a sense of stability. It wasn't much, but it was something.

As the years went on, John's need for structure grew with him. In high school he became the student who had every assignment color-coded and every project completed well before the deadline. His friends would joke about his obsession with planning, but for John, it wasn't a joke. It was survival. Every time he crossed something off his to-do list, every time he checked off another day that went according to plan, he felt a small measure of relief. It was like building a wall between himself and the chaos he had grown up with—a wall that, in his mind, would protect him from ever experiencing that kind of uncertainty again.

Another defining moment happened when John was sixteen. His parents had another fight, this one worse than any he had witnessed before. His father stormed out of the apartment, shouting that he was leaving for good. His mother collapsed on the couch, too tired and defeated to stop him. John stood frozen, watching his father walk out the door and out of their lives for the last time.

The door slammed shut, and any illusion of stability John had left was gone too. That night he promised himself that when he had a family, it would be different. He would be different. He would have a plan. He would be the one who kept everything together, who made sure nothing was left to chance. There would be no uncertainty, no chaos, no arguments about money, no walking out. His family would never know the kind of instability he had grown up with.

This need for control, born from the chaos of his childhood, became a core part of who John was. It shaped every decision he made as an adult. He planned everything—his career, his finances, his relationships—with the same precision he had once used to organize his school supplies. It wasn't just about order; it was about safety. It was about making sure that nothing could unravel the life he had worked so hard to build.

So when his wife, the free-spirited Sarah, tried to "disrupt his carefully constructed plans with her so-called fun" (John's words, not mine), it wasn't just frustrating for John; it was terrifying. He couldn't understand how she could live without a plan, how she could make decisions on a whim and leave so much to chance. To him, her spontaneity felt like a threat, a return of the chaos he had spent his entire life trying to escape. He didn't see it as freedom; he saw it as danger. It didn't even occur to him that she could be organized at work and unstructured at home.

But during that session when John finally opened up to Sarah about his childhood—about the arguments, the uncertainty, the night his father walked out—something was different. For the first time, Sarah understood the weight that John had been carrying all these years. She saw that his need for control wasn't about stifling her or limiting their life together—it was about keeping their life safe, about ensuring that they never went through what he had gone through as a child.

As John shared his story, Sarah's paradigm shifted. The label "controlling" began to crumble, replaced by a deeper understanding of the man she had married. She no longer saw his structure as an attack on her freedom; instead, she saw it as a shield he had built to protect them both. And in that moment, she realized that this wasn't just about John—it was about the scared little boy inside him who had spent his whole life trying to keep the chaos at bay.

What Sarah came to realize in that session—and what many of us miss in our own relationships—is that planning wasn't John's weapon. It was his shield. It wasn't about domination; it was about protection. Every calendar block, every color-coded plan, every backup strategy was rooted not in a desire to overpower but in what John thought was love. A fierce, loyal, and deeply committed love that had been formed, unknowingly, by fear.

Fear is a quiet sculptor. It shapes how we speak, how we plan, how we connect. Left unexamined, fear doesn't necessarily scream—it whispers. It tells us lies like, *If you don't plan everything, everything will fall apart.* Or, *If you let go, you'll lose everything.* And most dangerously, *If you relax, you'll become your father.*

John didn't set out to be an over-planner. He set out to be different. But in his effort to escape the chaos of his past, he inadvertently began to let fear write the script of his present. That's what fear does: It distorts love into something rigid, anxious, and self-protective. It disguises survival as responsibility. It turns safety into strategy. And in doing so, it often pushes away the very people we're trying to hold close.

According to psychologist Susan David, "Avoiding discomfort is the path to disconnection. Emotional agility—the ability to recognize, name, and work with our emotions—is what leads to growth."[3] John's discomfort with unpredictability wasn't just a quirk, it was unspoken grief. A childhood wound that had never healed. Once Sarah saw that, the man she had labeled "controlling" looked more like someone trying, desperately, to love her well. He had been doing it with the only tools he knew.

This is the question for all of us: What if the people who frustrate us most are not failing us but protecting themselves? What if the behaviors we criticize are actually biographies in disguise? What if fear, unspoken and unresolved, has been guiding our relationships more than we realized?

Only when we slow down to ask, "What happened to you?" instead of, "What's wrong with you?" can we truly begin to understand. And only then can we move from protection to connection, from fear to freedom.

IDENTIFYING AND EMBRACING OUR UNIQUENESS

Once the mask of behavior is removed and the fear beneath it is named, we're left with something far more sacred—our story. And within that story we begin to uncover the roots of our uniqueness. But discovering what makes us *us* isn't always easy. Sometimes it requires a deep, introspective journey into the moments that shaped us, the experiences that left imprints on our soul.

John's story is a powerful reminder that much of who we are is shaped by our past—by the experiences we lived through, by the roles we were asked to take on, and by the moments that defined us. For John, it was the chaos of his childhood that led him to seek structure and organization. It was not just a preference; it was a survival strategy. And for years he carried that need into every part of his life, especially into his relationship with Sarah.

Like John, we all have defining moments that shape us. But here's the challenge: most of us don't take the time to reflect on them. We don't stop to ask ourselves why we act the way we do, or why certain things matter so much to us. It's only when we dig deeper, when we look at the moments that have shaped us, that we begin to understand our uniqueness and how that uniqueness has been molded by our experiences.

Think about a time when you felt most in your element. Maybe it was a moment at work when you were leading a team, organizing a project, or creating something new. What did that moment say about who you are? Like John, whose past pushed him toward structure, you might find that your most natural tendencies—whether toward leadership, creativity, organization, or flexibility—are rooted in the experiences of your past. The key is to look back at those moments and start connecting the dots.

Maybe, like John, you grew up in an environment where there was little predictability. Perhaps you were the one who had to step up and create order out of chaos, and now, as an adult, you find comfort in planning and structure. Or maybe your uniqueness lies in creativity; perhaps you were encouraged to express yourself through art or music, or perhaps creativity was your way of escaping a rigid, structured upbringing. Whatever it is, the experiences of your past have not only shaped your personality but also highlighted the gifts God has given you.

Discovering your uniqueness might mean looking at your role in relationships. Are you more of a peacekeeper, the one who smooths over conflicts and brings people together? Are you a visionary, always thinking about the future and pushing for new ideas? Or are you one who thrives more on details, ensuring that nothing slips through the cracks? To be clear, you may be more than one of these; the question is which one you tend to lean more heavily on. These tendencies often stem from the roles you were asked to take on as a child, in school, or in early relationships.

John's story doesn't end with him understanding his need for organization: He began to see that his uniqueness, while valuable, also needed balance. He learned that his need for structure was not inherently bad, but that it had to be paired with an openness to Sarah's free spirit. That's when real growth happened for both of them.

The same is true for you. Once you understand your uniqueness, the next step is to take ownership of it. It is not enough to simply know why you are the way you are. You have to embrace it. God did not create you with your specific traits by accident. Your strengths, your mannerisms, your ways of thinking and processing the world—they are all part of his design for you. But understanding your uniqueness is just the beginning. The real challenge comes when you have to learn how to bring that uniqueness into harmony with the people around you.

If you're not sure where to start, there are helpful tools that can guide you on this journey. Personality and strengths-based assessments like the CliftonStrengths (formerly StrengthsFinder), Myers-Briggs Type Indicator (MBTI), or the Enneagram can give insight into how you're wired. Free online tools such as spiritual gifts assessments can help clarify how God has uniquely equipped you to serve. And if you want to go deeper, working with a spiritual director, spiritual coach, or therapist can help you reflect on formative experiences, explore patterns of behavior, and better integrate your story into your relationships.

In fact, it's often through those guided conversations that we start to see clearly—not just who we are, but *why* we are. If you're willing to do the work, the reward is worth it: clarity, confidence, and compassion for both yourself and the people around you.

FROM SELF-AWARENESS TO RELATIONAL WISDOM

Embracing your uniqueness is only half the journey. The other half—perhaps the more difficult and sacred half—is learning to embrace the uniqueness of others. It's one thing to understand the story behind your own behaviors, but it takes courage and compassion to pause and consider the story behind someone else's. When we begin to see that every person, like us, is shaped by hidden hopes, old wounds, and defining moments, we shift from reacting to relating. The challenge, then, is not just to own our biography, but to honor theirs.

Once John understood his need for structure, the next step was learning to embrace what he perceived as Sarah's free spirit. This wasn't an easy process. At first John's instinct was to resist, to feel frustrated by Sarah's spontaneity. After all, her way of living felt like the very chaos he had spent his whole life trying to avoid. But something shifted when John realized that Sarah's differences were not a threat—they were a gift. Her creativity, her ability to live in the moment (even though she was extremely organized), brought a joy and beauty to their life that his planning could not. Instead of seeing Sarah's spontaneity as something that needed to be fixed, he began to see it as something that could add to their relationship. And once he stopped resisting their differences, their relationship deepened. They were no longer fighting against each other's uniqueness; they were learning to balance them.

Now think about your own relationships. Maybe you, like John, have been frustrated by someone whose strengths seem to clash with yours. Perhaps you are someone who thrives on structure, but you have a child or spouse who is more free-spirited. Or maybe you are the more creative one, and your partner is the one who prefers order and predictability. It's easy to label these differences as obstacles, but what if, like John and Sarah, you saw them as opportunities for growth?

Take parenting as an example. Let's say you're the kind of parent who values discipline and order, and your child seems to push against every rule you set. It's frustrating because you've worked hard to create structure, and it feels like your child is constantly rebelling against it. But what if, instead of trying to force them into your mold, you took a step back and tried to understand why they are wired this way?

Maybe your child is more like Sarah—someone who thrives on creativity and freedom. Their resistance to structure isn't about defiance; it's about needing space to explore their world. When you approach their behavior with curiosity instead of frustration, you open up a new way of understanding them. Instead of labeling them as "rebellious" or "difficult," you begin to see that their differences are part of their uniqueness. And once you understand that, you can start to work with them in a way that honors their strengths while still teaching them the value of discipline.

This same principle applies to your relationships at work. Imagine you are part of a team where everyone has a different way of approaching problems. Maybe you are the detailed planner, while your coworker is the risk taker who is always pushing for bold ideas. It's easy to feel frustrated by the different approaches, but what if you started to see those differences as the key to innovation? Just as in John and Sarah's relationship, it is the tension between differing perspectives that leads to growth. The risk taker helps you think outside the box, while your attention to detail ensures that the ideas are grounded in reality.

And here's where it all comes together: Learning to embrace others' differences requires empathy and humility. Instead of assuming you know why someone behaves a certain way, ask. Be open to hearing their story, just as Sarah eventually heard John's. When Sarah learned about John's chaotic childhood and understood why structure mattered so much to him, it changed the way she saw him. She no longer saw his planning as controlling; she saw it as a way for him to feel safe. In turn, John became more willing to loosen his grip on control because he no longer felt misunderstood. The same shift can happen in your relationships. When you take the time to understand the why behind someone's behavior, the labels you've placed on them—controlling, lazy, distant—begin to fall away. You start to see them as they are: people shaped by their own unique set of experiences, fears, and desires.

The truth is, relationships thrive not when we force others to conform to our way of thinking, but when we learn to balance our strengths with theirs. Just as John and Sarah's relationship deepened when they embraced their differences, your relationships can flourish when you stop fighting against the uniqueness of those around you. Whether it is your spouse, your children, or your coworkers, the key is to approach their differences with curiosity, empathy, and a willingness to learn from them. In doing so, you create space for understanding and connection.

This process is not always easy. It requires a willingness to step outside your own perspective and make room for someone else's. It means being vulnerable enough to ask the hard questions— "Why do you need this?" "Why does this matter to you?"—and listening to the answers without trying to change them. It also means accepting that the things that frustrate you about someone else might not be flaws but strengths you haven't yet learned to appreciate.

As you begin to do this, something remarkable happens: you become more adaptable. Instead of fighting against the differences in your relationships, you learn to flow with them. You begin to see how your strengths and someone else's perceived weaknesses, or vice versa, can complement each other, creating a balance that makes your relationship stronger. It's like two pieces of a puzzle that, on their own, seem incomplete, but when brought together, form a beautiful picture.

There will still be moments of frustration, moments when the differences feel like too much, but instead of resisting them, you can begin to see them as opportunities for growth. Just as iron sharpens iron, it is the friction of differences that sharpens us, making us more resilient, more empathetic, and more connected to each other. Every time you choose to embrace the uniqueness of someone else, you are choosing growth—not just for yourself, but for your relationship.

And here's the truth: you will never fully understand someone else's story, just as no one will fully understand yours. But that doesn't mean you can't seek to know each other more deeply. It doesn't mean you can't appreciate the beauty in their differences or find ways to celebrate the qualities that make them who they are.

When you approach your relationships—whether with a spouse, child, or colleague—with a heart open to understanding and embracing differences, you create the space for something extraordinary to happen. You create the space for real connection, for mutual respect, and for love that goes beyond surface-level understanding. And in doing so, you not only grow as an individual, but you also help those around you grow into the fullest expression of who God created them to be.

PONDER POINTS

1. What labels have you placed on others that may be blinding you to their deeper story?

2. Where might fear—yours or theirs—be showing up in your communication, masked as control, silence, or frustration?

3. How would your relationships change if you asked "What happened to you?" instead of "What's wrong with you?"

4. In what ways might your own past be shaping how you show up in conflict? And what parts of your story still need healing?

5. Who have you misunderstood simply because you didn't pause long enough to listen beyond their behavior?

PRAYER

God, help me to see beneath the surface. Teach me to recognize that every behavior carries a story and behind every wall is a person longing to feel safe. Soften my heart where I've judged too quickly, and open my ears to hear what isn't being said. Heal the fearful places in me that push others away. Give me wisdom to name my own wounds and grace to love others through theirs. May I become someone who listens deeply, loves patiently, and leads with compassion. Amen.

5

FROM COLD WARS TO CLOSE HEARTS

WHAT IF THE silence in your relationship isn't peace, it's war with the volume turned down?

For many couples, conflict doesn't explode. It freezes. It starts not with yelling but with withdrawal—the long pauses, the loaded silences, the casual "I'm fine" that carries the weight of a hundred unmet needs. The real danger to a relationship often isn't the clash of strong personalities but the slow drift of unspoken tension. The cold war, not the loud battle, is what quietly freezes connection. Over time, hearts that once felt close begin to grow distant—not because love is gone, but because misunderstanding has taken its place.

Here's the good news: distance doesn't have to mean disconnection. In this chapter, we explore practical, grace-filled strategies for transforming tension into teamwork, starting with tools that don't just resolve conflict but invite you back into intimacy and mutual respect. From the "yes, and" technique to the biblical wisdom behind repair and grace, you'll discover that differences don't have to divide—they can become the very place where deeper love is built. Because when handled with care, even the coldest war can give way to closeness.

When couples reach out for help, they're often handed tools that barely scratch the surface, strategies that sound wise in theory but fall flat when the heartache runs deep and the differences feel immovable. We're often told that the keys to a healthy relationship are things like active listening and setting boundaries. And while those practices matter, they don't always go far enough—especially when you're staring across the dinner table at someone who sees the world completely differently than you do. In the thick of relational conflict, advice like "just listen better" can feel like being handed a Band-Aid for a broken bone.

Real growth happens when we learn how to engage with difference—not just tolerate it, but actually work with it. That means developing strategies that don't shut the other person down, but instead create space for both perspectives to be honored. And that's where one of the most transformative tools I've seen comes in, something called the "yes, and" technique.

The concept comes from the world of improv comedy, where performers are trained to never reject what a scene partner says. Instead, they build on it, responding with, "Yes, and . . ." to keep the story moving forward. It's not just a stage trick; it's a mindset shift. Instead of contradicting, you collaborate. Instead of canceling out someone's perspective, you make room for it while still expressing your own.[1]

According to research from the Gottman Institute, one of the most consistent predictors of a successful relationship is the ability to turn toward your partner's emotional cues rather than away from them.[2] That doesn't mean you have to agree with everything they say—it means you acknowledge their experience as valid. Psychologist Susan Johnson, founder of Emotionally Focused

Therapy, calls this kind of emotional attunement "the primary pathway to bonding and repair."[3]

Let me show you how this works in real life. I once worked with a couple—let's call them Marcus and Tasha—who were at their breaking point. The tension between them had grown so intense that almost every conversation ended in an argument. Tasha felt that Marcus wasn't emotionally available, while Marcus felt that Tasha's constant need to discuss her feelings was overwhelming. They were locked in a cycle: Tasha would bring up an issue, Marcus would shut down or try to "fix" it, and Tasha would feel unheard. Every attempt at communication seemed to widen the gap between them.

One day, in a particularly heated session, Tasha was expressing her frustration about how Marcus never seemed to be truly present when she wanted to talk. "You always have one foot out the door when we're talking," she said. "It's like you're just waiting for me to finish so you can go do something else. I feel like you don't care."

Marcus's immediate instinct was to defend himself. His body language stiffened, and I could see the words forming on his lips: "That's not true." In his mind, he was already preparing a rebuttal, ready to argue that he did care and that Tasha's perception was wrong. But I stopped him.

"Marcus," I said, "instead of focusing on what you disagree with, try to find something in what Tasha just said that you can agree with. Something small, something that resonates."

Marcus paused. He was visibly frustrated, but after a moment of silence, he nodded. "Okay. Yes," he said, turning to Tasha. "I understand that it seems like I'm not fully there when we talk. And I can see how that would make you feel like I don't care."

That shift—moving from "No, you're wrong" to "Yes, and"—was a breakthrough. Tasha's face softened, and I could see the tension in the room begin to lift. For the first time, Marcus wasn't dismissing her feelings; he was acknowledging them. He wasn't agreeing with everything Tasha was saying, but he was accepting the part he could understand, and from there, he was able to build a bridge.

Once Marcus had accepted Tasha's perspective, he was able to add his own: "And the reason it seems like I'm not fully there is that I get overwhelmed when we have these conversations. I don't always know how to respond, so I pull away. But I do care, and I want to be better at showing you that."

The shift in their dynamic was immediate. By using the "yes, and" technique, Marcus wasn't just avoiding conflict, he was creating space for a deeper connection. He wasn't focused on defending his point of view or proving Tasha wrong. Instead, he validated her feelings, which opened the door for him to share his own. And in that moment, Tasha felt heard. Instead of escalating the argument, they were able to move the conversation forward.

Tasha, in turn, responded with her own "yes, and."

"Yes," she said, "I can see how these conversations might be overwhelming for you. And I think we can work on finding a way to talk that feels less intense for both of us."

Through this simple but profound technique, they were able to transform what had started as a defensive, tense exchange into an opportunity for deeper understanding. They weren't necessarily agreeing on everything, but by starting with the common ground of "yes," they were able to build on each other's perspectives rather than tearing them down.

The "yes, and" technique works because it reframes the conversation. Instead of focusing on what you disagree with—on the gap between your perspectives—you start with what you can agree on, even if it's something small. This doesn't mean you're ignoring the differences. It means you're choosing to acknowledge the other person's reality before offering your own. The "yes" is an invitation to understanding, and the "and" is where you add your perspective, allowing for a more productive, compassionate dialogue.

Imagine how this approach could change the way you handle conflict in your own relationships. Think about the last disagreement you had, whether with a spouse, a friend, or a coworker. How did it start? Most conflicts begin with one person making a statement and the other immediately offering a rebuttal. But what if, instead, the next time you're in a disagreement, you start with "yes"? What if, instead of trying to defend your point of view, you first look for a way to acknowledge the truth in what the other person is saying?

Let's say you're in a heated debate with a friend about a political issue, and they say something you strongly disagree with. Instead of immediately countering with "No, that's not true," you say, "Yes, I see why that would be important to you, and I also think we should consider this other perspective." Suddenly, the conversation shifts from a battle of wills to a collaborative exchange of ideas. The tension eases, and both parties feel heard and respected.

The "yes, and" technique doesn't erase differences, but it makes room for them. It creates a safe space where both people can express their views without fear of being shut down. And when that space is created, real communication happens. This is the essence of navigating irreconcilable differences: not eliminating them, but learning how to use them as opportunities for connection and growth.

"Yes, and" is just one strategy for navigating conflict. While it works to build connection in the heat of the moment, it's not the only way we can shift the narrative in our relationships. Often, differences run deeper than a single conversation or an isolated argument—they touch on the core of who we are, how we process the world, and what we've experienced in the past. And when conflicts begin to spiral, we need more than techniques to smooth over the surface. We need tools to get to the heart of the issue.

That's where deeper strategies, rooted in both research and biblical principles, come in.

Take, for instance, the concept of repair attempts, which John Gottman identifies as a crucial factor in healthy relationships.[4] A repair attempt is any gesture, big or small, that signals an intention to reconnect after a conflict. It might be a touch on the arm, a soft laugh to break the tension, or even a simple, "I'm sorry." It's an act of grace acknowledging that the relationship is more important than being right.[5]

This idea echoes a central biblical truth about grace and forgiveness. Proverbs 15:1 reminds us, "A soft answer turneth away wrath: but grievous words stir up anger." Repair attempts, much like the grace we are called to extend to one another, can defuse anger and bring us back into harmony.

Let's shift to a workplace scenario. Imagine two coworkers, Jasmine and Layla, who are on the same team at work. Jasmine would describe herself as detail-oriented, someone who makes sure every project is flawless before it gets submitted. Layla is more of a big-picture thinker, focused on meeting deadlines and getting things done quickly, even if it means sacrificing some of the finer details.

Their different work styles create ongoing tension. Jasmine feels that Layla is careless and rushed, while Layla thinks Jasmine is slowing the team down by being overly meticulous. Their clashes become a constant source of frustration, not just for them but for the entire team. Their disagreements often escalate into passive-aggressive comments or heated exchanges during team meetings.

One afternoon, the tension between them hits a breaking point. They have been tasked with submitting a high-priority project, and the deadline is looming. Jasmine, as usual, wants to spend more time perfecting the final draft, while Layla is adamant that they needed to submit it immediately. The argument begins to spiral, with both digging their heels in. Layla snaps, "You're always slowing things down! We're going to miss the deadline because of you!"

Jasmine fires back, "At least I care about the quality of our work, unlike you!"

The project—and their professional relationship—seems on the verge of collapse.

But in that heated moment, Jasmine takes a deep breath and makes a repair attempt. She looks at Layla and says, "I'm sorry for being so harsh. I know I can be slow with projects sometimes, but I just want us to submit something that's really solid. I don't mean to frustrate you."

That small acknowledgment—an apology without strings—shifts the energy in the room. Layla, still visibly tense, softens just a little. "I get it. I just feel like we're going to miss the deadline if we don't move fast. And that stresses me out. But I know you care about the details."

This moment of grace from Jasmine allows both women to step back from the edge. Instead of continuing to attack each other, they find a way to compromise. Jasmine suggests that they submit the project on time but schedule a quick review the next day to make any final edits. Layla, feeling seen and respected, agrees. The project gets submitted, and they are able to move forward without lingering resentment.

That moment of grace, that repair attempt, is a reminder of how God calls us to extend kindness and gentleness in our interactions. Just as Jasmine acknowledged Layla's stress, repair attempts in our relationships give us the chance to remind each other we're on the same team.

But repair attempts alone aren't enough. We also need to become fluent in what Gottman calls emotional "bids," those subtle cues we give each other in daily life that signal a need for connection, reassurance, or support.[6] They can be as obvious as a request for help or as quiet as a sigh, a glance, or a question like, "Did you see that?" How we respond to those bids—whether we turn toward, turn away, or turn against—plays a pivotal role in the strength and resilience of our relationships.

Let's return to Jasmine and Layla.

As they continue collaborating, Jasmine notices that every time a tight deadline approaches, Layla fidgets—tapping her pen, avoiding eye contact, moving restlessly. These aren't just nervous habits. They are emotional bids, Layla's unspoken way of saying, "I'm feeling overwhelmed. Do you have my back?"

Once Jasmine learns to recognize these signals, she begins responding differently. One afternoon, with the deadline looming, she leans over and says, "I can tell this deadline's stressing you out. Let's look at what we've got so far—I think we're closer than it feels." That small gesture—the bid met with presence—changes everything. It softens Layla's anxiety, builds trust, and strengthens their partnership.

These small moments when we choose to turn toward instead of away are the bedrock of emotional connection. As Gottman's research shows, couples who consistently respond to each other's bids for connection have a much higher chance of staying together—not because they avoid conflict, but because they stay emotionally attuned in the midst of it.[7]

But what if you're always the one doing the attuning? What if you're the one who always notices the tension, always reaches across the gap, always meets the emotional bid—but rarely feels seen yourself?

It's a valid question. And it's one many might resonate with, especially those in relationships where emotional labor feels uneven. Dr. Thema Bryant, psychologist and president of the American Psychological Association, puts it this way: "Love should not be a one-person performance. Relationships thrive when emotional responsibility is shared—not just held by the one with the most awareness."[8]

Responding to emotional bids is a beautiful expression of care, but it's also a shared responsibility. One-sided attunement can lead to burnout, even resentment. If you find yourself always being the "emotionally available one," it may be time to have a loving but honest conversation: "I want to keep showing up for you. But I also need to know you're showing up for me."

God does call us to sacrificial love, as we see in Ephesians 5:25. But sacrifice in Scripture is never about martyrdom—it's about mutual flourishing. So yes, keep turning toward the people you love. But don't lose yourself in the process. Healthy connection does not mean carrying it all alone. It means co-creating a relationship where both people learn to name their needs, listen deeply, and respond with grace.

When we bring together these strategies—repair attempts, responding to emotional bids, and sacrificial love—we are equipped to connect across what might feel like insurmountable differences. These aren't just conflict-resolution tools; they are expressions of the grace, love, and wisdom God calls us to embody in all our relationships. In embracing these practices, we aren't just resolving conflict; we are becoming more like Christ, who always seeks reconciliation, always turns toward us, and always loves us sacrificially.

Say What You Feel, Without Wounding

Once you've begun to turn toward each other and repair what's been broken, the question becomes: how do we stay connected? There are more tools we can use to bridge the gap when our differences seem to drive us apart. One of the most powerful methods is nonviolent communication (NVC), a technique developed by psychologist Marshall Rosenberg. NVC is a four-part process designed to foster compassionate dialogue without blame, shame, or coercion.[9] It aligns closely with the biblical principles of kindness, patience, and humility found in Ephesians 4:29: "Let no corrupt communication proceed out of your mouth, but that which is good to the use of edifying, that it may minister grace unto the hearers."

NVC involves four key steps:

1. Observation: Describe what is happening without judgment or interpretation.

2. Feeling: Express how you feel in response to what you observed.

3. Need: Identify the need that is behind the feeling.

4. Request: Make a request for what you would like to happen, without demanding it.

Let's say you've been feeling disconnected from your spouse because they've been spending more time at work and less time with you. Instead of saying, "You never make time for me," which is likely to make your spouse defensive, you could try an NVC approach: "I've noticed you've been working late a lot this week (observation). I'm feeling lonely and a bit neglected (feeling), because I need quality time together (need). Would you be willing to schedule a dinner with just the two of us sometime this weekend?" (request).

Notice how this approach focuses on your feelings and needs rather than blaming your spouse. It invites them into a conversation where they can respond without feeling attacked, making it more likely that you'll reach a positive resolution. NVC encourages both parties to be vulnerable and honest, which fosters deeper understanding and connection. This approach isn't limited to romantic relationships; its principles can be applied in various contexts, even in friendships where communication challenges often go unnoticed until they build up.

For example, a young lady, Tamara, came to me for advice on how to improve communication with her significant other. She had felt unheard and dismissed in their relationship, and she wanted practical strategies to be able to express herself without feeling shut down. We spent time working on different ways she could approach her partner, but during one session, Tamara casually shared a situation that had happened over the weekend while she was out with her girlfriends.

She told me that during dinner with these friends, one of them was being loud, making bold jokes, and taking over the conversation. Tamara, who is more reserved, found herself feeling irritated. "She just couldn't stop talking," Tamara said, shaking her head. "I was ready to leave halfway through the night, and by the time we got home, I didn't even want to talk to her."

I could tell by Tamara's tone that this wasn't just about her friend's behavior at dinner; it was deeper. She felt unseen in the friendship. Tamara hadn't expressed her frustration to her friend, but the tension was building.

I introduced Tamara to the concept of nonviolent communication, suggesting that maybe her friend's behavior wasn't just about being loud or dominating the conversation. I asked her, "What if your friend's need to talk is actually her way of seeking validation from the group, or just her way of trying to feel connected? Could there be an underlying need there that you've been overlooking?"

This is the essence of NVC: shifting the focus from the person's actions to the need behind the actions. I explained to Tamara that NVC teaches us to communicate through four steps: observing what's happening, sharing our feelings, expressing the needs behind those feelings, and making a request that invites connection.

I then encouraged Tamara to reframe her frustration using NVC in her next conversation with her friend. Instead of focusing on the "loudness," she could start with an observation like, "Kyra, at dinner the other night, I noticed you were really leading the conversation." Then she could share how it made her feel: "I felt a little left out." From there, she could express her need: "I need a little more space to contribute in our conversations." And finally, she could make a request: "Could we try to make more room for me to speak next time?"

Tamara agreed to try it out. A week later she came back with an update. She had invited Kyra to coffee and, after a little small talk, gently brought up how she had been feeling. "I did what you said," Tamara told me, "and it worked." She shared with Kyra how she had been feeling at dinner without making Kyra feel blamed or attacked. To Tamara's surprise, Kyra had opened up about how she sometimes felt pressure to entertain everyone in the group, especially when she was nervous. Tamara's approach using NVC allowed them to have an honest conversation where both women felt heard.

This is the power of nonviolent communication—it invites connection instead of division. By focusing on the needs behind the behavior, Tamara was able to communicate her feelings without blame, which allowed Kyra to share her own vulnerability. Their friendship grew stronger because Tamara chose empathy over judgment, and Kyra was able to meet her halfway.

Nonviolent communication, when practiced with intention, helps us move from reactive, defensive responses to understanding and compassionate dialogue. It reflects Christ's call to engage each other in love, seeking not to tear down but to build up. The simple act of acknowledging the other person's needs can transform even the most challenging relationships.

But what happens when we don't catch ourselves in time? What happens when, instead of listening and responding with empathy, we allow miscommunication, frustration, and unchecked emotions to fester? No relationship is immune to conflict, but when we fail to address the core needs behind our behavior, our differences can lead to disconnection rather than unity.

This disconnection doesn't happen all at once. It creeps in through small moments—an ignored emotional bid here, a sarcastic remark there—until, before we know it, our once-healthy relationship feels strained and unrecognizable. In these moments we begin to see the emergence of what Gottman calls the Four Horsemen of the Apocalypse: criticism, contempt, defensiveness, and stonewalling.[10]

Left unchecked, these four destructive habits can tear apart even the most solid relationships. They chip away at the foundation of trust and love, turning minor misunderstandings into insurmountable obstacles. And if we aren't intentional about countering them, they can lead to a place where reconciliation feels impossible. We will look more closely at the horsemen in the next chapter.

PONDER POINTS

1. Where has silence crept into your relationships, and what might it be covering up? Are there "cold wars" happening that need warmth, words, or grace to break the ice?

2. Which tool from this chapter—"yes, and," repair attempts, emotional bids, or nonviolent communication—do you most need to practice right now? What's one relationship where this could make a difference?

3. Have you been the one constantly turning toward, repairing, and attuning without feeling reciprocated? What would it look like to lovingly express your need to be seen too?

4. When you think about your past conflicts, how often did fear lead the conversation instead of love?

5. How can you begin shifting from defensiveness to curiosity in future interactions?

6. What would it mean for you to love sacrificially without losing yourself?

7. How can you embrace empathy without becoming emotionally overextended?

PRAYER

God of restoration and reconnection, you are the one who bridges the greatest chasm—between our brokenness and your wholeness. Teach us to do the same in our relationships. Help us to turn toward each other with compassion, not retreat in silence or strike with sharp words. Give us the courage to repair what's been strained, to respond with gentleness, and to speak truth wrapped in grace. When we are misunderstood, steady our hearts. When we are overwhelmed, remind us that love can still lead. When differences feel like barriers, open our eyes to the beauty they hold. Let your Spirit guide us into humility, emotional wisdom, and sacred connection. And in every conversation—especially the hard ones—may we reflect your kindness, patience, and peace. In Jesus' name, amen.

6

THE ANATOMY
OF DISCONNECTION

THE DAY IS ETCHED in my memory. It was one of those quiet, unassuming evenings where everything on the surface felt normal. The boys were asleep, the house was still, and my ex-wife and I were sitting at the kitchen table. It should have been a simple conversation, maybe about bills or the kids, but something had been building between us for a while. The air was thick with words unspoken.

I don't remember how it started, but I remember how it ended. I said something—maybe about work, maybe about how exhausted I felt—and that's when she looked at me with a sadness I couldn't place and said, "You don't see me."

I didn't even know what she meant by that. I froze, defensively thinking, *What are you talking about? I'm here, aren't I?* I wanted to say, "Of course I see you. Why else would I have worked so hard to try to keep this family together, to provide, to be present?" But I stayed silent, feeling the weight of her words hit me like a blow.

Her words weren't meant to hurt. But they did. For the first time, I realized our disconnect went far deeper than surface disagreements. It wasn't just about bills, chores, or responsibilities—it was more than that. She wasn't talking about physical sight; she was talking about emotional blindness. Somewhere along the way I had stopped seeing her—who she was, what she needed, what she was trying to communicate.

At the time, I didn't understand. I took it personally, thinking she was criticizing me, accusing me of failing as a husband. My immediate instinct was to defend myself. But what she needed wasn't my defense—she needed my understanding, my presence, and my willingness to see her for the person she was, not just for the roles she played.

That moment at the kitchen table was a turning point, though I didn't realize it then. It was one of the last real conversations we had before everything started to unravel. And now, when I look back, I can see the signs so clearly—the patterns we fell into, the way we talked past each other rather than to each other, the mounting frustrations neither of us could name.

What I didn't realize at the time was that we were trapped in a cycle, one I would later come to understand as the Four Horsemen of the Apocalypse.

THE FOUR HORSEMEN OF FAILED RELATIONSHIPS

In relationships—whether romantic, familial, or platonic—there are patterns of communication that can quietly corrode even the strongest connection. Dr. John Gottman, a leading researcher on marriage and relational stability, calls them the Four Horsemen of the Apocalypse: criticism, contempt, defensiveness, and stone-walling.[1] These behaviors don't always show up in obvious ways. They creep in gradually—through sighs, sarcastic jabs, defensiveness masked as logic, or long silences that stretch just a little too far—until the emotional distance between two people feels unbridgeable.

At first glance, these patterns often look like fundamental personality differences. When every conversation feels like a battle and every disagreement ends in a standoff, it's easy to believe the issue is incompatibility. Maybe we just see the world too differently. Maybe we want different things. Maybe these differences can't be overcome.

But here's the deeper truth: what often feels like overwhelming difference is really relational misalignment, a breakdown in the way two people are communicating, interpreting, and responding to one another's needs.

It's not the presence of conflict that determines the fate of a relationship, but how conflict is managed.[2] As Gottman explains in *The Seven Principles for Making Marriage Work*, 69 percent of conflicts in relationships are perpetual, meaning they won't go away. The difference between successful and struggling relationships isn't the absence of problems but the presence of repair, grace, and healthy communication patterns.[3]

These four horsemen are not personality flaws; they are relational symptoms, warning signs that communication has shifted from connection to protection, from understanding to self-defense.

Contemporary therapist and researcher Dr. Sue Johnson, founder of Emotionally Focused Therapy, taught that the strongest relationships are not those without conflict, but those where partners feel safe enough to show vulnerability and repair emotional disconnection.[4] So before we label ourselves as "too different to survive" in a relationship, we must ask: Is this really about differences? Or is it about disconnection we haven't yet learned how to heal?

To answer that question honestly, we have to slow down and examine the habits that have taken root in our communication.

Because disconnection doesn't always announce itself with shouting or slamming doors. Sometimes it hides in the everyday exchanges—the way we make a request, respond to frustration, or shut down mid-sentence. These subtle patterns, if left unchecked, become relational defaults. And among the most destructive of these is the first of the four horsemen: criticism.

On the surface, criticism looks like a clash in values or perspectives. One person wants things done one way; the other wants something entirely different. But beneath that criticism is often an unexpressed need, a feeling of being overwhelmed or unappreciated. When I criticized my ex-wife for how she handled things at home, it wasn't because I thought her way of doing things was wrong. Deep down, I was frustrated because I felt like I was carrying a burden alone, but I didn't know how to say that. So instead of communicating my feelings, I lashed out.

Criticism isn't about the dishes or the bills or the laundry—it's about feeling unseen, unheard, or unvalued. But because we don't have the tools to communicate those deeper emotions, criticism becomes our weapon of choice. It feels like we're fundamentally different, but in reality we're missing connection, failing to communicate what's really going on beneath the surface.

Criticism is a silent assassin. It can sneak in under the guise of "constructive feedback," but over time it becomes more insidious. It's not just about pointing out a behavior; it's about attacking the person's character.

I think back to that night at the kitchen table. When I said, "What more do you want from me?" it wasn't a genuine question. It was a criticism disguised as frustration. It was my way of saying, "I'm doing everything, and you're doing nothing." Criticism goes beyond addressing the issue—it digs into the person, making them feel inadequate. Instead of saying, "I feel overwhelmed with the bills," I made it about her, implying she wasn't doing enough.

You've likely seen this in your own life. Maybe you've found yourself saying things like, "Why do you always leave the dishes out?" or "You never listen to me." These aren't just observations, they're criticisms that make the other person feel attacked. And when criticism becomes a regular part of your communication, it sets the stage for something even more dangerous: contempt.

If criticism is a seed, contempt is the poisonous plant that grows from it. Contempt shows up as sarcasm, eye-rolling, name-calling, or mocking. It's the act of putting yourself above the other person, of making them feel less-than. Contempt is often fueled by long-standing resentment or unresolved issues that have built up over time.

In that same conversation with my ex-wife, I remember a moment when she sighed and said, "I'm so tired of this." But it wasn't the words that hurt, it was the tone. It was the roll of her eyes, the way she made it clear that I was a burden, that this conversation wasn't worth her time. Contempt creates distance. It tells the other person, "You're not worth the effort."

Contempt is one of the most toxic forces in any relationship. It leads to bitterness, and once bitterness takes hold, it can be difficult to eliminate it. You might recognize it in your own relationships—maybe in a sarcastic comment during an argument or an exasperated sigh when your partner makes a mistake. Over time, these seemingly small gestures erode the bond of trust and respect that relationships are built on. When you feel misunderstood or dismissed for too long, contempt becomes the armor you wear to protect yourself from further hurt. It's not that you don't care anymore, it's that caring has become too painful. And so contempt comes out, not because you're too different to get along, but because you've lost the ability to see each other through the lens of grace.

When criticism and contempt are in play, it's only natural for defensiveness to follow. Defensiveness is another horseman that disguises itself as irreconcilable differences. It looks like both people are standing their ground, unwilling to admit fault or compromise. But defensiveness is rarely about stubbornness for its own sake. It's about fear—fear of being wrong, fear of being blamed, fear of being misunderstood. When I defended myself in that conversation with my ex-wife, I wasn't really fighting her. I was fighting the fear that I wasn't enough. The fear that I was failing as a husband. My defensiveness wasn't about our differences, it was about my insecurities and my inability to open up about what I was really feeling.

You've probably seen this play out in your own life. Maybe it was during a conversation with your partner about something that seemed small at first, like not helping around the house enough. Your partner says something like, "I feel like I'm doing everything by myself." Immediately, your defenses go up.

You might say, "I've been busy too. You know how hard work has been. I'm trying my best."

But even as the words leave your mouth, you know the conversation has taken a turn. What could have been an honest moment of connection now feels like a battle. Your partner wasn't trying to say you don't do anything. They were expressing how overwhelmed they feel, hoping you might understand and offer support. But instead of listening to the feeling behind their words, you focused on defending yourself, on making sure they knew your side of the story.

This is how defensiveness creeps in. It feels like self-protection, but what it really does is shut down any chance of meaningful dialogue. You're no longer talking about the issue at hand; you're talking about why you're not to blame. And in doing so, you're blocking the connection that could come from truly hearing the other person's perspective.

Or maybe it happens with a close friend. You've been drifting apart lately because of busy schedules and life's demands, and suddenly, you're not texting as much. Your friend brings it up, maybe during a catch-up lunch: "I've noticed we haven't been hanging out as much. Are we okay?"

Your heart sinks a little. You didn't even realize how much time had passed. But instead of acknowledging it, you say, "Well, you haven't exactly been reaching out either. I'm always the one making plans." Now the conversation has shifted. Instead of addressing the initial concern—your friend's feelings of distance—you've made it about your effort versus theirs. Defensiveness has turned what could have been a chance to reconnect into a back-and-forth about who's been the better friend. And in that moment, the chance to truly hear each other is lost.

Maybe this is your life at work. Your boss approaches you and says, "You didn't loop me into that project update, and it's caused some confusion." Instantly your mind races to justify. You respond, "I didn't have time; I was juggling three other tasks." And while that might be true, the defensiveness prevents you from really hearing the impact your actions had. Instead of owning a small misstep, you've shifted the conversation to explain why it wasn't your fault. And now, instead of working through the issue, both sides feel frustrated.

Defensiveness shows up in all kinds of relationships—romantic, friendships, professional. It's the gut reaction we have when we feel blamed, and instead of leaning into the conversation to understand where the other person is coming from, we focus on protecting ourselves. And by doing that, we make it nearly impossible to address the real issue at hand.

Imagine what could happen if, in those moments, instead of reacting defensively, you took a breath. When your partner says, "I feel like I'm doing everything by myself," you could respond with, "Yes, I can see how that would feel overwhelming, and I didn't realize you were carrying so much on your own. Let's figure out how we can tackle things together." Or when your friend mentions the distance between you, instead of deflecting, you could say, "Yes, I understand how you'd feel like we've grown apart, and I realize I haven't been as present. I'm sorry if it seemed like I was pulling away."

Even in a work setting, when your colleague points out an oversight, instead of defending yourself, you could use the "yes, and" technique we discussed earlier. "Yes, I can see how that caused confusion, and I'll make sure to keep you in the loop next time."

Remember, by starting with "yes" and building from there, you're not just agreeing for the sake of agreeing; you're acknowledging the other person's feelings and adding your own perspective to move the conversation forward. Instead of focusing on what's wrong, you're focusing on what's possible, and that shift can change the trajectory of any conversation.

When the first three horsemen—criticism, contempt, and defensiveness—take over, the fourth often follows: stonewalling. Stonewalling is the act of shutting down completely, of withdrawing from the conversation entirely. It's the refusal to engage, to even acknowledge the other person's feelings. It's the silent treatment, the cold shoulder, the emotional wall that keeps the other person out.

Psychologist Harriet Lerner, author of *The Dance of Anger*, explains that emotional withdrawal can be deeply destabilizing. When one partner shuts down, the other may feel like the ground beneath them has disappeared. According to Lerner, it's not always disagreement that harms a relationship but the emotional unavailability and lack of responsiveness that create lasting damage.[5] Stonewalling, then, becomes less about disagreement and more about disconnection, a signal that one person feels so overwhelmed that disengagement feels like the only option left.

Imagine this: You're sitting at the dinner table with your partner after a long day. You're not arguing, but you've brought up a topic that's been weighing on you—maybe something about feeling disconnected lately, or how you've been carrying a lot of the household responsibilities. You're calm, trying to express yourself without sounding accusatory, but as soon as the words leave your mouth, you notice a shift.

Your partner doesn't respond. They're still sitting across from you, but the body language changes. They pick up their phone, scrolling aimlessly, or maybe they just stare off into the distance. You're mid-sentence, but it's as if the conversation has ended before it even began. You try again, offering more explanation, hoping to get some kind of response, but the silence remains. No eye contact, no acknowledgment, just an empty, quiet space where connection should be.

It's not an argument. It's not heated. But the silence? It's deafening. And it leaves you feeling . . . invisible. Like your words don't matter. Like you don't matter.

That's stonewalling. It's the slow withdrawal, the shutting down of communication not in anger but in avoidance. And the more you try to engage, the more distant your partner becomes. No yelling, no walking out the door—but they're not present either. Your partner is right there in front of you, but emotionally they're a million miles away.

If you've ever been on the receiving end of this, you know how isolating it can be. It feels like there's an invisible wall between you, a barrier you can't break through no matter how hard you try. You're left wondering, *What did I do wrong? Why won't my partner talk to me?*

The good news is, the person stonewalling often isn't intentionally doing so. It's not about ignoring you or not caring, it's often about being emotionally overwhelmed. Maybe the topic feels too heavy, or they don't know how to respond. Maybe they're afraid of where the conversation might lead, and shutting down feels like the safest option. It's their way of coping, but for you, it feels like rejection.

This was the case with a couple I worked with—let's call them Taylor and Jordan. Taylor often found herself in conversations with Jordan that went exactly like this. They'd be talking about something simple—maybe planning a trip or discussing a decision for the house—and out of nowhere Jordan would go quiet. Taylor would be midconversation, and suddenly Jordan would zone out, pick up his phone, or just nod along without really engaging. It wasn't aggressive, but it felt like an emotional door was being slammed shut.

At first Taylor didn't understand what was happening. She felt ignored and dismissed, like Jordan wasn't even trying to connect. But through our sessions, we uncovered that Jordan wasn't trying to hurt Taylor; he was overwhelmed. Jordan had grown up in a household where conversations often led to conflict, and over time he learned to avoid confrontation by simply shutting down. It wasn't that Jordan didn't care about the relationship, it was that he didn't know how to stay present without feeling emotionally flooded.

Once Taylor realized this, everything changed. She stopped taking the silence personally and started seeing it as a sign that Jordan needed space. They began using a simple strategy: when Jordan started to shut down, instead of pushing the conversation forward, Taylor would say, "It seems like this is a lot right now. Let's take a break and come back to it." This gave Jordan the space he needed to process without feeling pressured to respond immediately.

For Jordan, the key was learning to recognize when he was stonewalling and finding ways to express his need for space rather than shutting down. Sometimes that meant taking a five-minute break during a conversation to collect his thoughts. Other times it meant agreeing to revisit the topic the next day, when he felt more emotionally equipped to engage. Over time they began to trust that the conversation wouldn't escalate into conflict, and Taylor learned that sometimes a pause could be more productive than pushing through the silence.

Stonewalling doesn't look like a dramatic argument. It's much more subtle. It happens in the quiet moments, in the silences that stretch too long, in the distant gaze or the mindless scrolling. And while it might seem harmless at first, over time that silence creates emotional distance, leaving both people feeling disconnected.

But stonewalling isn't an insurmountable barrier. It's a signal, a sign that the conversation needs to slow down, that emotions need space to breathe. When we recognize stonewalling for what it is—an emotional flood, not an emotional withdrawal—we can create room for reconnection. Sometimes the best thing you can do is give each other the grace of space. Step back, breathe, and then re-engage when both of you are ready to communicate openly again.

Stonewalling often feels like an irreconcilable difference and extreme distance because it shuts down the very thing relationships rely on: communication. In Taylor and Jordan's case, it created a silent barrier where Taylor felt dismissed and Jordan felt overwhelmed. But what's really happening beneath the surface is a need for emotional regulation. Jordan wasn't withdrawing to hurt Taylor—he was retreating because he felt emotionally flooded and unable to continue the conversation without feeling overwhelmed.

The first step in breaking this cycle is recognizing that stonewalling isn't a failure of love; it's a response to emotional overload. It's the body's way of saying, I need space. While that space might feel like abandonment to the other person, it's actually a plea for time to regain emotional stability. But here's the challenge: relationships can't thrive on silence alone. Partners must find a way to come back into the conversation once the emotions have settled.

For Taylor and Jordan, we worked on introducing a simple but effective strategy, what we called "time-outs." Instead of Jordan silently shutting down midconversation, we created a signal that would allow him to step away and collect his thoughts. Something as simple as saying, "I need a break" gave both of them clarity. This allowed Jordan to retreat without triggering feelings of abandonment in Taylor, while giving Taylor reassurance that Jordan wasn't disappearing for good—just taking a moment to breathe.

The time-out strategy helped them reframe their communication. Taylor learned that Jordan's silence wasn't about rejecting her or dismissing her concerns, it was his way of asking for emotional space. And Jordan learned how to communicate his need for that space in a way that didn't leave Taylor feeling alone. It wasn't an immediate fix, but over time their relationship strengthened as they began to trust that stepping back for a moment didn't mean stepping away for good.

If you've ever experienced stonewalling—whether you're the one shutting down or the one on the other side of that silence—know that it doesn't have to be the end of the conversation. Silence might feel like a wall, but it can also be a doorway if you're willing to find a way back into dialogue. The key is recognizing when emotional overload is happening and giving each other the grace to step back, breathe, and then re-engage once the emotional tide has settled.

Stonewalling doesn't mean the relationship is doomed, but it does mean that both partners need to work on emotional awareness and communication. It's about learning to say, "I need a minute," instead of disappearing into silence. It's about finding ways to stay connected, even when the emotions feel too big to handle in the moment. And most importantly, it's about coming back—because silence on its own can't heal, but honest conversation can.

By embracing this space in communication, like Taylor and Jordan did, you open up a path to understanding. And through that path, you find a way to use moments of emotional overwhelm not as barriers, but as opportunities for growth.

INTERRUPTING THE CYCLE OF DISCONNECTION

Recognizing the four horsemen is the first step in breaking the cycle. Each of these behaviors—criticism, contempt, defensiveness, and stonewalling—can be countered with healthier communication strategies. But it takes intentional effort and a willingness to be vulnerable. It takes acknowledging when we've fallen into these patterns and committing to doing better.

We can replace criticism with a gentle startup—expressing our feelings without attacking the other person. Instead of saying, "You never listen to me," we can say, "I feel unheard when we have conversations like this."

Contempt can be countered with gratitude and appreciation. Instead of focusing on what the other person is doing wrong, we can make an effort to acknowledge what they're doing right. This shifts the tone of the relationship and helps rebuild respect.

Defensiveness can be overcome by taking responsibility for our actions, even if only for a small part of the conflict. Instead of saying, "I didn't do anything wrong," we can say, "I can see how my actions might have hurt you, and I'm sorry for that."

Stonewalling can be broken by taking breaks during intense conversations to calm down and then re-engaging with a clearer mind. This prevents the emotional shutdown that comes with feeling overwhelmed.

By recognizing and addressing these four destructive habits, we can stop the cycle of broken communication before it destroys the relationships we value most. And in doing so, we reflect the love, patience, and grace God calls us to embody in our interactions with others.

Let's not forget that relationships aren't destroyed overnight. They are slowly worn down by the small, everyday choices we make—to criticize instead of encourage, to withhold instead of express, to defend instead of listen. But just as relationships are worn down by these choices, they can be rebuilt through small, intentional acts of love and understanding. We have the power to break the cycle.

PONDER POINTS

1. Which of the four patterns—criticism, contempt, defensiveness, or stonewalling—do you recognize in your own relationships, and what might be underneath it?

2. Consider what unspoken emotions, fears, or needs might be driving these responses.

3. When have you chosen protection over connection?

4. Reflect on moments when you shut down, lashed out, or defended yourself instead of leaning in. What would a "yes, and" response have looked like?

5. What small step can you take this week to interrupt a negative pattern? It could be as simple as offering gratitude instead of sarcasm, pausing when you feel defensive, or gently saying, "I need a moment to process."

PRAYER

God, you see every place where my relationships feel strained or stuck. Help me name the habits that are harming connection—and give me the humility to change them. Teach me to speak gently, to listen deeply, and to love in a way that reflects your grace. Where I have caused distance, let me be a bridge. Where I have shut down, open my heart again. Thank you for being a God who always turns toward me, even when I don't know how to respond. Amen.

7

WHY WE LOVE THE WAY WE DO

Before we learn how to love, we learn how to survive. And for many of us, survival started early. In the living room where a parent's silence spoke louder than words. At the dinner table where our needs were too inconvenient to acknowledge. In bedrooms filled not just with toys but with tension—the kind you can't name, only feel. Long before we entered romantic relationships, friendships, or marriages, we were students of emotional safety. We studied what triggered an outburst, what invited affection, and what earned disapproval. And we adapted, not because we were broken, but because our brains were built to protect us. This is the hidden curriculum of childhood trauma.

The term *adverse childhood experience* (ACE) comes from a groundbreaking study by the Centers for Disease Control and Kaiser Permanente in the late 1990s that revealed a profound connection between early emotional wounds and long-term physical, emotional, and relational outcomes. These experiences range from the obvious—physical abuse, parental addiction, domestic violence—to the often-overlooked: emotional neglect, chronic unpredictability, or the quiet ache of growing up with a caregiver who simply didn't know how to be present.[1]

What makes ACEs so impactful is not just what happened but how those experiences rewired our understanding of love, trust, and connection. Neuroscience confirms that chronic stress in childhood, especially within the context of unstable caregiving, alters the development of the brain's stress-response system, leaving individuals more prone to anxiety, hypervigilance, and emotional dysregulation later in life.[2]

In short, trauma doesn't end when childhood does. That child who learned to suppress their tears becomes the adult who shuts down in conflict. The child who tiptoed around a volatile parent becomes the partner who fears disagreement. The one who never felt emotionally seen may now crave intimacy—and fear it in the same breath.

Most of us don't recognize these patterns as trauma echoes. We call them personality clashes, irreconcilable differences, or simply "the way I am." But beneath many of our most frustrating relational behaviors lie unhealed wounds. And until we face those wounds with honesty and compassion, we'll keep trying to solve adult problems with child-sized tools.

In this chapter, we explore how ACEs and early attachment styles shape the way we show up in relationships. We walk through the invisible weight childhood trauma places on adult love. And most importantly, we begin to name what was never named in our past, so we can finally stop reliving it in our present.

As psychiatrist Bessel van der Kolk reminds us, "The body keeps the score," but healing begins when we learn to read the story.[3] To begin reading the story, we have to start with the parts that are easiest to miss—the wounds that left no bruises, the absences that spoke volumes. Trauma doesn't always arrive with violence or catastrophe. Sometimes it comes quietly, through what wasn't said, what wasn't offered, or what we never had the permission to need. One of the most overlooked, and most deeply shaping, forms of childhood trauma is neglect.

NEGLECT: THE TRAUMA OF ABSENCE

Neglect, as defined by the Centers for Disease Control and Prevention, is "the failure to meet a child's basic physical and emotional needs," including food, shelter, affection, safety, supervision, and emotional nurturance.[4] Unlike abuse, which tends to leave visible marks, neglect leaves behind questions: *Was I not worth noticing? Was I too much—or not enough—to be cared for?*

What makes neglect so insidious is its invisibility. There's no clear-cut moment of impact, no singular event to point to. Instead, it's the ongoing absence of what should have been present—of soothing, attention, affection, and responsiveness. Psychiatrist Bruce Perry emphasizes that neglect is not the mere absence of something; it is the absence of enough of the right things at the right time.[5]

Children are biologically wired for connection. When that connection is inconsistent or missing, the brain interprets it as danger. Over time, this lack of responsiveness wires the child's nervous system for survival rather than security. Dr. van der Kolk explains that children who grow up in neglectful environments often "learn to disconnect from their bodies, their needs, and even their memories" in order to cope.[6]

There was a woman named Candace, who as a child had food, clothing, and a roof over her head—but never had anyone to talk to. Her parents were overwhelmed with their own issues: mental illness, long work hours, and generational trauma. No one ever asked Candace how she was doing. No one noticed when she was sad or praised her when she succeeded. She wasn't hit. She wasn't screamed at. But she was invisible.

As an adult, Candace carried that invisibility into every relationship. She struggled to express her needs, often telling partners she was "fine" even when she felt abandoned or overwhelmed. Deep down, she didn't believe her feelings mattered. In conflict, she would withdraw, not to punish, but because she had learned early on that no one would come anyway. She didn't fear being yelled at; she feared being dismissed.

Research confirms that neglect is one of the most damaging forms of trauma. According to the original ACE study, children who experienced neglect—especially emotional neglect—were significantly more likely to develop depression, anxiety, and attachment issues later in life.[7] And unlike some other traumas, neglect often goes unacknowledged by the person who experienced it, making it even harder for healing to begin.

But here's the good news: healing starts with recognition. When we name the silence for what it was—a wound, not a weakness—we begin the work of restoration. Psalm 34:18 reminds us, "The LORD is nigh unto them that are of a broken heart; and saveth such as be of a contrite spirit." God does not dismiss the invisible wounds. He draws near.

ABUSE: WHEN LOVE AND SAFETY COLLIDE

If neglect is the trauma of absence, abuse is the trauma of betrayal. It is what happens when someone entrusted with our care becomes a source of pain. Abuse—whether physical, emotional, or sexual—violates not only the body but the spirit. It disrupts the foundational belief that love is safe, that the people closest to us can be trusted.

Abuse and neglect can be defined as "the actions or inactions of an individual's caregiver or parent inflicting physical, sexual, or emotional harm on the individual."[8] That harm can be overt, like a slap or a scream. But it can also be subtle and chronic—words that diminish, stares that shame, silence that isolates.

There was a guy named Darien whose father never hit him, but rarely missed an opportunity to cut him down. "You're so sensitive," his dad would scoff when Darien cried. "Quit acting like a girl." When Darien showed excitement about art or music, he was told to "man up" and "focus on something that matters." Praise was reserved for toughness. Weakness was mocked. Over time, Darien stopped sharing who he was. He didn't stop feeling, he just stopped expressing.

By the time he reached adulthood, Darien was successful by all appearances. A good job. A polished demeanor. But he struggled in relationships. Any time his partner brought up a complaint, even gently, he would shut down or explode. He wasn't trying to be difficult, he was trying to protect himself from shame. His body remembered the sting of every belittling word, and it responded with defense.

Emotional abuse like what Darien endured is often harder to recognize but no less damaging. It rewires the brain's stress responses and teaches children that affection is conditional and identity is unsafe. Dr. Steven Stosny explains that emotional abuse is more insidious than physical violence because it systematically breaks down self-worth.[9]

Meanwhile, physical abuse sends a different but equally destructive message: "You are not safe." Children exposed to physical harm often develop what researchers call a hypervigilant nervous system—a brain that's always on high alert. Even in calm

environments, they may perceive threat, misread tone, or antic-
ipate abandonment.[10] This makes conflict in adult relationships
feel life-threatening, even when it's about something as small as
leaving dishes in the sink.

And then there's sexual abuse, which is not just a violation of
boundaries but a violation of being. Survivors often carry deep
shame, confusion, and a severed connection between their body
and their sense of self. They may struggle with intimacy, trust, or
the ability to feel safe in their own skin. Survivors of abuse are not
broken, but they often carry a deep longing for safety that can't be
easily named.

All forms of abuse undermine a child's basic developmental
needs: safety, stability, and unconditional love. When those
needs are violated, the child often internalizes the abuse as a
reflection of their own worth: If someone I love hurt me, maybe
I deserved it.

But hear this: You did not deserve it. No child ever does.

The ACE study found that children who experienced abuse
were far more likely to suffer from depression, anxiety, addiction,
and relational struggles later in life.[11] The pain may have happened long ago, but its echoes often show up in our most intimate relationships, especially when we are triggered, hurt,
or afraid.

And yet Scripture reminds us that God is not absent in our pain.
The psalmist writes, "He healeth the broken in heart, and bindeth
up their wounds" (Psalm 147:3). Abuse may have shaped part of
your story, but it does not get the final say. Healing is possible.
Reclaiming your voice, your worth, and your sense of safety is not
only possible, it's holy.

Connecting with Somone Who
Has Experienced Abuse

Connecting with someone who has been abused requires more than good intentions—we must approach these relationships with emotional attunement, deep empathy, and a commitment to creating safety. Abuse fractures a person's sense of trust, leaving behind invisible wounds that shape how they experience relationships. Whether the abuse was physical, emotional, sexual, or verbal, the common thread is this: Someone they trusted violated their dignity. Rebuilding trust, then, becomes a delicate process, one that must move at the survivor's pace, not our own.

One of the most important ways to foster connection with a survivor is to create emotional safety. According to Dr. Judith Herman, a leading trauma expert, "Recovery can take place only within the context of relationships; it cannot occur in isolation."[12] But those relationships must be consistent, predictable, and non-judgmental. Survivors need to know that you will show up—not just once, but again and again—with steady, compassionate presence. Emotional safety doesn't mean avoiding hard topics; it means creating an environment where the survivor knows they will not be shamed, pressured, or rushed.

It also means learning to listen without trying to fix. Survivors have often had their experiences minimized or disbelieved. Many have heard things like, "Are you sure it was that bad?" or "Maybe you're overreacting." When they open up, what they need most is not advice, it's validation. Simply saying, "I believe you" or "That should never have happened to you" can be profoundly healing. As trauma therapist Laura van Dernoot Lipsky writes, "Being deeply heard is often the first real experience of justice for survivors."[13]

Your role is not to rescue them but to reflect their dignity back to them, to be a mirror that says, "I see you. You matter."

Respecting boundaries is also essential when connecting with someone who has experienced abuse. Because abuse often involves the violation of personal or emotional space, survivors may have a heightened sensitivity to being controlled or coerced, or even to well-meaning intrusiveness. For example, asking too many probing questions or pushing someone to share before they're ready can retraumatize rather than support. Instead, offer choices and let them set the pace: "You don't have to talk about anything unless you want to. I'm here when you're ready." This communicates that they have agency—something abuse may have stripped from them.

I worked with a young man named Jamal who had experienced years of emotional abuse from a parent. As an adult, he struggled with deep-seated shame and a strong need to stay in control. In our early conversations, he was guarded and quick to shift topics. Rather than push, I focused on creating an environment where he didn't feel pressured to open up. Over time, as he saw that I would show up consistently and without judgment, his guard began to lower. One day he said, "I'm not used to people just being okay with me being quiet. It's like you're not trying to fix me." That moment became a turning point. What broke through his walls wasn't force, it was patience.

Affirming a survivor's dignity is one of the most powerful ways to rebuild trust. Abuse often plants lies about identity, lies that say, "You're broken," "You're hard to love," or "You're not enough." When you see them through the lens of worth and value, you become part of the healing. Instead of focusing solely on their pain, reflect their strength. Remind them that surviving was an act of courage. Author and therapist Beverly Engel emphasizes that one of the most damaging effects of abuse is the loss of self-worth. Restoring that sense of worth must be at the center of healing.[14] Sometimes, that restoration begins with a simple sentence: "You're still here. That's not weakness—it's resilience."

Finally, while you can be a source of support, it's important to know your role. You are not a therapist, but you can be a bridge to deeper healing. If the survivor is open, offer to help them find a therapist, counselor, support group, or spiritual mentor. The work of healing is sacred, and God often uses community as a vessel for restoration.

In the end, connecting with someone who has experienced abuse means creating a safe space and being someone who doesn't demand performance but offers presence. It means learning to see beyond behavior and into the story behind it. And it means recognizing that love, when offered gently and consistently, can begin to mend what fear once fractured.

HOUSEHOLD DYSFUNCTION: WHEN HOME ISN'T A SAFE PLACE

Not all childhood wounds come from what was missing. Some come from what was always there—the volatility, the secrets, the sound of a slammed door that made your heart race even before you understood why.

Household dysfunction is a form of trauma that disrupts a child's internal sense of safety and stability. Unlike neglect, which is about emotional absence, household dysfunction is about emotional chaos. This chaos grows out of things like mental illness, substance abuse, chronic conflict, incarceration, or domestic violence. Even when a child's basic needs are met, the atmosphere of unpredictability can feel like living in a minefield: always alert, always bracing for the next emotional explosion.

For children raised in dysfunctional homes, the message is clear but unspoken: Love is conditional. Safety is fragile. Trust is dangerous.

Consider Malik, whose home always looked picture-perfect from the outside—yard trimmed, parents employed, dinner on the table. But inside? His father's drinking made every evening a gamble. Sometimes he was jovial; sometimes he was cruel. Malik learned early on to tiptoe, to scan for danger, to mediate fights between his parents before finishing homework. He became emotionally fluent not because someone taught him, but because no one protected him. Now, as an adult, he finds himself overfunctioning in relationships, afraid that any sign of tension will lead to collapse. He assumes responsibility for everyone's emotions, yet he feels exhausted and unseen.

Dr. Bruce Perry explains that children growing up in homes marked by emotional chaos often develop a heightened stress-response system. Their brains become wired to detect danger rather than to connect emotionally. "Survival trumps reflection," Perry writes. "You can't think your way out of terror. You have to feel your way back to safety."[15]

This is why adults from dysfunctional homes might struggle to relax in healthy relationships. Not walking on eggshells feels unfamiliar, maybe even unsafe. Silence triggers panic. Calm feels like the quiet before a storm. Some become hyper-responsible, trying to control everything and everyone to avoid the chaos they once endured. Others emotionally check out because they've learned that being present only leads to pain.

What makes household dysfunction particularly insidious is how easily it hides behind the mask of "normal." There may be family photos on the wall and prayers at dinner—but behind closed doors, children are left to manage grownup emotions in child-sized bodies. That's not love. That's survival.

The gospel offers us something better. Psalm 46:1 says, "God is our refuge and strength, a very present help in trouble." For those of us shaped by dysfunction, healing begins with remembering that we were never meant to parent our parents. We were never meant to be the emotional regulators of the household. We were children who needed care. And through God's grace, we can begin to unlearn the patterns of hypervigilance, emotional suppression, and codependency that once kept us alive but now keep us disconnected.

DIVORCE: WHEN A CHILD'S WORLD SPLITS IN TWO

When a child's home falls apart, their sense of stability, safety, and self often fractures with it. While some adults view divorce as a rational solution to an unhealthy relationship, children frequently interpret it through a more fragile lens: "If love can fall apart, how do I know anything is secure?"

According to the CDC-Kaiser ACE study, parental separation or divorce is one of the original ten adverse childhood experiences linked to long-term health and behavioral outcomes.[16] While the legal end of a marriage might mark closure for parents, for a child, it often introduces confusion, divided loyalties, and chronic emotional tension. Research shows that children of divorced parents are more likely to experience mental health challenges, increased anxiety, relational trust issues, and difficulty regulating emotions in adulthood.[17]

Let's go back to the story of Malik. Whenever he and his wife argued, no matter how minor the disagreement, Malik's body went into panic mode. "I just feel like everything is going to fall apart," he confessed. "Like one wrong word will be the end of us." As we talked, it became clear that Malik wasn't just reacting to his wife—he was reliving the fear he'd felt as a child when his parents divorced after a series of explosive fights. He had never learned to trust that conflict could lead to resolution rather than destruction.

Malik's story is not uncommon. Children who experience divorce often develop what psychologists call a hypervigilant attachment system: They're constantly scanning for signs of abandonment, interpreting neutral feedback as rejection, and fearing that conflict equals catastrophe.[18] Their emotional thermostat is set to "survival," and unless that setting is recalibrated through healing, it can affect every future relationship.

This is why Scripture speaks so clearly about God's heart for the brokenhearted. Psalm 27:10 says, "When my father and my mother forsake me, then the LORD will take me up." For those who grew up in homes fractured by divorce, this verse offers profound hope: God steps in when the very foundations of love seem to collapse. He becomes the anchor when everything else feels uncertain.

But even with this divine assurance, healing takes time. As adults, children of divorce must often learn new relational scripts that aren't based on fear, avoidance, or emotional shutdown. They must relearn how to trust, how to stay present in conflict, and how to believe that love can endure even through disagreement.

Understanding divorce as an ACE helps us approach people bearing these wounds with compassion instead of confusion.

When someone flinches at conflict, pulls away emotionally, or questions the permanence of love, we can ask not, "What's wrong with them?" but "What happened to them?" That shift—from judgment to empathy—is where healing begins.

Emotional instability in the home is another form of trauma that can be insidious. A child who grows up in a volatile environment, where a parent's mood swings dictate the emotional climate of the home, learns to walk on eggshells. Like other ACE survivors, they become hyper-aware of their surroundings, constantly scanning for signs of danger or emotional outbursts. This can result in anxiety and a heightened stress response that carries into adulthood, making it difficult to relax or feel safe in relationships. For example, an adult who grew up in this kind of environment might interpret a partner's frustration as a sign of impending abandonment, reacting with either over-apology or withdrawal as a defense mechanism.

When we think of trauma, it's easy to focus on the big, dramatic events, but these more subtle forms of trauma can be just as destructive. Children are incredibly perceptive, and even small, seemingly inconsequential experiences—like hearing a parent yell at a sibling or being left out of family decisions—can leave lasting imprints. The cumulative effect of these small traumas often leads to deeply ingrained emotional and psychological patterns that we carry into adulthood. As the CDC-Kaiser research revealed, individuals with a high number of ACEs are more likely to experience difficulties with emotional regulation, trust, and communication in adulthood.[19] These challenges are often at the root of what we perceive as irreconcilable differences in relationships.

I've seen this dynamic play out in many of the couples and individuals I've coached. In many cases, irreconcilable differences aren't born out of a lack of love or compatibility; they emerge from the unhealed wounds people carry from childhood. These wounds manifest in behaviors that can seem impossible to reconcile on the surface, but when we look deeper, we often find that these differences are cries for healing, connection, and understanding.

The Hidden Weight of Trauma

Imagine you're in a relationship where every disagreement seems to turn into a crisis. Even minor misunderstandings trigger an intense emotional response that feels disproportionate to the situation. You're left confused and frustrated, wondering why the person you love can't seem to manage conflict in a healthy way. Beneath that reaction likely lies a history of trauma—early experiences of instability, neglect, or fear that have shaped the individual's emotional responses and coping mechanisms.

Maya grew up in a home filled with constant emotional instability. Raised by a single mother who struggled with substance abuse, Maya often found herself caring for her younger siblings and acting as a buffer in adult conflicts. In the chaos of her childhood, she learned to cope by withdrawing emotionally, retreating into herself to survive the emotional storms swirling around her. Fast-forward to her adult relationships, and this pattern of withdrawal became a major source of tension. Whenever conflict arose, whether over finances or household responsibilities, her instinct was to shut down. To her partner, this looked like stonewalling, a refusal to engage. But for Maya, it was a deeply ingrained response rooted in trauma.

We know from the ACE study that childhood trauma can rewire the brain. The constant stress and unpredictability of growing up in a chaotic environment can cause the brain's stress-response system to go into overdrive. This leads to hypervigilance and an exaggerated "fight, flight, or freeze" response in adulthood. Maya's withdrawal during conflict wasn't about her partner at all—it was about the unhealed wounds from her childhood. She had developed an emotional survival strategy that helped her cope in the chaos of her upbringing, but in her adult relationship, it created distance and misunderstanding.

Maya's partner grew up in a household where conflict was swept under the rug. His parents avoided confrontation at all costs, modeling a passive approach to disagreement. As a result, he learned to fear conflict, equating it with danger. When Maya withdrew during arguments, he felt abandoned, fearing that the relationship was falling apart. This was a direct result of his own adverse childhood experience—a subtle yet powerful form of trauma that taught him that conflict was something to be feared rather than faced.

The result was that Maya and her partner both saw conflict not as something to be solved but something to escape from or avoid. Maya's withdrawal and her partner's anxiety about it led to differences that felt irreconcilable, but when we explored these dynamics through the lens of ACEs, they became understandable.

It's important to note that ACEs don't just affect relationships; they affect every aspect of life. The CDC-Kaiser study revealed that individuals with four or more ACEs are at a significantly higher risk for mental health disorders, chronic illness, and substance abuse later in life.[20] These long-term effects are also seen in how people form and maintain relationships. For those who carry unresolved childhood trauma, even minor conflicts can trigger overwhelming emotional responses, making it difficult to navigate disagreements in a healthy way.

In the face of these differences, we must remember that healing is possible. God never intended for us to remain trapped in the patterns of our past. While trauma may shape our present, it does not have to dictate our future. The Bible tells us in 2 Corinthians 5:17, "Therefore if any man be in Christ, he is a new creature: old things are passed away; behold, all things are become new." This means that through Christ, we are given the opportunity to break free from the cycles of our past and to embrace a new way of relating to others.

For Maya and her partner, healing began when they acknowledged the trauma that was shaping their behaviors. By understanding how their ACEs were influencing their emotional responses, they were able to show each other more grace and compassion. They learned to approach conflict with curiosity rather than defensiveness, recognizing that their differences weren't signs of incompatibility but reflections of their unique histories.

Through prayer, counseling, and open communication, they began to break the patterns that had once felt impossible to overcome. With God's grace, the very differences that had once caused them to feel distant became opportunities for deeper connection and growth.

HEALING THROUGH GRACE AND UNDERSTANDING

In your own relationships, you may be facing differences that feel irreconcilable. Perhaps your partner reacts to conflict in ways that seem unreasonable, or perhaps you find yourself withdrawing when things get tough. Whatever the case, it's important to remember that trauma often shapes our differences. And while trauma can create challenges in relationships, it also provides an opportunity for growth and healing.

The key to navigating these differences lies in becoming aware of our trauma wounds and approaching our relationships with compassion. When we acknowledge the impact of ACEs, we can begin to shift our perspective—seeing the scars that shape us and the grace that can heal us.

PONDER POINTS

1. What unspoken messages did your childhood teach you about love, safety, and worth? How might those messages be shaping your relationships today?

2. Consider whether your reactions in conflict or intimacy are rooted in past patterns of survival rather than present trust.

3. When you think about your partner's (or friend's) patterns of behavior, what parts of the wounded child might be driving the adult response?

4. How does trauma-informed compassion invite us to ask, "What happened to them?" instead of, "What's wrong with them?"

PRAYER

Lord, help me to see the wounds I carry with honesty and grace. Heal the places in me that still ache from what I didn't receive, and teach me to love others not through the lens of fear, but through the freedom you offer. Make me new in you. Amen.

8

THE ROOTS BENEATH
THE REACTION

Parenting Styles and Emotional Triggers

As we consider the impact of childhood trauma on adult relationships, we must also turn our attention to another critical factor: parenting styles. The way we were parented leaves an indelible mark on how we relate to others, often without us even realizing it. The rules and boundaries—or lack thereof—that shaped our childhoods can lay the groundwork for how we navigate love, conflict, and connection in adulthood. Parenting is not just about discipline. It's the framework through which we learn about security, trust, and communication.

When we face what seem like irreconcilable differences in relationships, we can often trace the roots back to the parenting styles we experienced as children. Whether we grew up in a home with strict rules, too much freedom, or not enough support, those early experiences shape how we engage in our adult relationships.

There are generally four types of parenting styles: authoritarian, authoritative, permissive, and neglectful. Each one has its own way of shaping a child's understanding of love, discipline, and emotional expression. Let's explore how each of these styles can affect us later in life.

AUTHORITARIAN PARENTING:
THE WEIGHT OF PERFECTION

In authoritarian homes, rules are strict and nonnegotiable. The message is clear: obedience is key, and failure to meet expectations often leads to punishment, disapproval, or emotional withdrawal. In these environments, love may feel conditional, something earned rather than freely given.

Take Layla, for instance. She grew up in a home where her father was the ultimate authority. His love seemed tied to her performance—good grades, proper behavior, everything had to be perfect. Mistakes were not met with understanding but with cold distance or harsh words. As a child, Layla learned that love and approval were things she had to work for, not something given unconditionally.

As an adult, Layla carried that mindset into her relationship with Darnell. In the early years of their marriage, she often found herself anxiously seeking his approval, constantly worried about whether she was "enough." If Darnell didn't compliment her cooking or acknowledge her efforts around the house, she'd spiral into feelings of inadequacy. To her, love meant performing and meeting invisible standards to keep the connection alive.

The impact of authoritarian parenting doesn't disappear when we become adults. Research shows that children raised in these environments often struggle with low self-esteem and anxiety, constantly questioning their worth. As adults, they may find it hard to trust that they are loved for who they are, not for what they do.

Layla's upbringing created a mindset where conflict felt like failure, and failure meant a loss of love. She wasn't just dealing with disagreements in her marriage, she was wrestling with the belief that if she wasn't perfect, she wasn't worthy of love.

PERMISSIVE PARENTING: LOVE WITHOUT BOUNDARIES

On the opposite end of the spectrum is permissive parenting—a style that's big on love but short on structure. In permissive homes, parents are nurturing and supportive, but they struggle to set boundaries. The child's desires often take center stage, and discipline is rare or inconsistent. The result is a lot of freedom but not much guidance.

Darnell, Layla's husband, grew up in a permissive household. His parents were warm and caring, but they didn't enforce many rules. If Darnell didn't feel like doing his homework, no one pushed him. If he broke curfew, his parents shrugged it off. While this created a sense of freedom, it also left Darnell without a clear understanding of boundaries or responsibility.

As an adult, Darnell found himself avoiding commitment and structure. In his marriage with Layla, this became a source of tension. He loved her deeply, but when it came to making plans for the future or following through on promises, he'd often drop the ball. Layla, who craved reassurance and stability, couldn't understand why Darnell seemed so laid back about things that felt important to her. And Darnell, used to a life without many boundaries, struggled to see why his casual approach was causing Layla so much stress.

Children raised in permissive households often grow up with a sense of entitlement or a lack of self-discipline. As adults, they may resist structure and find it difficult to manage responsibilities. In relationships, this can lead to conflicts where one partner feels like they're carrying all the weight while the other seems indifferent or disengaged.

The permissiveness of Darnell's upbringing made it hard for him to see the importance of boundaries, not just in life but in love. He wasn't intentionally avoiding responsibility; he had simply never learned how to embrace it.

AUTHORITATIVE PARENTING: THE BEST OF BOTH WORLDS

Then there's authoritative parenting, often considered the ideal balance. In these homes, parents set clear expectations but offer plenty of warmth and support. They encourage their children to be independent but also provide guidance when needed. Conflict is met with communication, not punishment, and love is unconditional.

Let's consider Jake and Alana. Alana grew up in an authoritative household where her parents were both firm and fair. There were rules, but there was also room for her to express herself. When she made mistakes, her parents didn't withdraw love—they used these moments as teaching opportunities, helping her understand the consequences of her actions without making her feel unworthy.

As an adult, Alana carried that confidence into her relationship with Jake. She wasn't afraid to set boundaries or ask for what she needed, but she did so in a way that respected Jake's feelings. When conflict arose, she approached it with calmness, knowing that disagreement didn't mean the end of the relationship. Alana understood that love wasn't conditional, and she brought that sense of security into her marriage.

Research shows that children raised in authoritative homes tend to grow up with high self-esteem, emotional resilience, and strong social skills. As adults, they are more equipped to handle conflict, express their needs, and build healthy relationships.

Alana's upbringing gave her the tools she needed to navigate differences without feeling threatened. She understood that conflict could be productive and that through communication, she and Jake could grow stronger together.

NEGLECTFUL PARENTING:
THE ABSENCE OF CONNECTION

Finally, we have neglectful parenting, where children are left to fend for themselves emotionally. Neglectful parents are neither responsive nor demanding, and this lack of involvement leaves children feeling ignored, emotionally abandoned, or even invisible.

One of the most heartbreaking examples is Eric. Eric grew up in a home where his parents provided for his physical needs but were emotionally absent. They didn't show much interest in his feelings or struggles. As a result, Eric learned to shut down his emotions and keep his distance from others. Vulnerability felt unsafe, and trust became something he struggled with throughout his life.

As an adult, Eric found it hard to form deep connections. He was often distant in his relationships, avoiding emotional conversations or brushing off his partner's attempts to get close. When conflict arose, his default was to withdraw, retreating into silence rather than engaging in the conversation. His partner felt frustrated and hurt, not understanding why Eric seemed so detached.

Children raised in neglectful environments often grow up with trust issues, difficulty in forming close bonds, and low self-esteem. As adults, they may struggle with emotional intimacy, finding it hard to open up or express their needs in relationships.

For Eric, neglect wasn't just something that happened to him in childhood, it became the framework through which he viewed all his relationships. He wasn't intentionally shutting his partner out, but his upbringing had left him with a deep fear of emotional vulnerability.

A Day at the Office: The Subtle Tensions of Parenting Styles

It was a typical Tuesday morning at Horizon Media, a digital marketing agency known for its fast-paced environment. The office hummed with the usual mix of chatter, keyboard clicks, and the occasional phone ringing. Marissa sat at her desk, her hands moving swiftly across her keyboard, her brow furrowed in concentration. She had a client meeting in an hour, and every detail of the proposal had to be perfect.

Across the room, Terrence, one of her colleagues, was leaning back in his chair, headphones over his ears, his eyes half-closed as he bobbed his head to the music. His desk was cluttered—papers, pens, and coffee cups stacked in a haphazard mess—but he didn't seem to notice. His approach to work had always been more relaxed, much to the frustration of Marissa, who thrived on organization and order.

The tension between them had been building for weeks. They were working together on a major campaign, but their styles couldn't have been more different. Marissa meticulously planned every step, creating detailed timelines and spreadsheets. Terrence was the kind of guy who would come up with a brilliant idea at the last minute, often bypassing the process Marissa had so carefully crafted.

Today, the tension reached a boiling point.

"Terrence, we're supposed to present to the client in an hour," Marissa said, trying to keep her voice calm as she walked over to his desk. "Have you finished the creative brief yet? I sent you the template last week."

Terrence glanced up, pulling one earphone off and looking at her like she was overreacting. "Relax, Marissa. I've got it covered. I'm working on something now."

Marissa blinked, momentarily thrown by his nonchalant tone. "Terrence, we're almost out of time. This is a huge client, and we need everything to be perfect. Why didn't you use the template I sent?"

Terrence shrugged, leaning forward and closing his laptop. "I don't need a template, Marissa. I've been doing this for years. You always freak out over the details, but I promise, it'll be fine. I just need a little space to work my magic."

Marissa's stomach twisted into knots. She could feel her pulse quicken as frustration bubbled to the surface. "Space to work your magic? This isn't a brainstorming session! We have a deadline, Terrence. The client is expecting a formal proposal, not one of your last-minute ideas that you throw together."

The tension in the air was thick enough to cut with a knife. Marissa's mind raced. She had been up half the night, double-checking every part of their presentation, making sure all the logistics were ironed out. For her, preparation was everything; it was what separated success from disaster. Terrence, on the other hand, seemed to operate in a world where deadlines were flexible, and "good enough" was the standard.

"Look," Terrence said, standing up from his chair and stretching his arms over his head, "I get that you like everything to be super organized, but that's just not how I work. We've got different approaches, and that's fine. You do your thing, and I'll do mine."

Marissa felt her chest tighten. She didn't want to lose her cool, but his laid-back attitude felt like a slap in the face. "Different approaches? Terrence, we're supposed to be a team! You can't just wing it every time and expect everything to fall into place."

Terrence smirked, raising an eyebrow. "Hasn't it always worked out in the end?"

Marissa could feel her hands trembling. She wanted to scream, but instead, she turned and walked back to her desk, biting her tongue. Inside, she was furious. How could he be so careless? How could he not see that his approach was reckless, that it put everything they had worked for at risk?

For the rest of the morning, the tension between them simmered. Marissa pored over her notes, double-checked the slides, and kept an eye on the clock, counting down the minutes until the meeting. Terrence, meanwhile, wandered over to the kitchen to grab another coffee, seemingly oblivious to the storm brewing just a few feet away.

Finally the meeting began. Marissa's portion of the presentation went off without a hitch—everything was polished, professional, and precise. But when it came time for Terrence to present his part, Marissa's worst fears were realized. His brief was incomplete, his ideas half-baked, and the client's faces quickly shifted from interest to skepticism.

As they left the meeting, Marissa couldn't hold it in anymore.

"I can't believe you just did that," she said, her voice shaking with frustration. "You completely ignored everything we worked on. That was a disaster."

Terrence ran a hand through his hair, his laid-back demeanor slipping just for a moment. "Marissa, calm down. It wasn't that bad."

"Not that bad? Are you serious? I stayed up half the night working on this, and you just . . . winged it."

Terrence sighed, his shoulders slumping. "I didn't mean to mess it up. I just . . . I didn't see the point in stressing over every little detail like you do. That's not how I work."

Marissa stared at him, feeling a wave of exhaustion wash over her. "But Terrence, this isn't just about how you work. We're a team. We need to respect each other's approaches if we're going to succeed."

Now, here's the question: based on their behaviors, can you guess the parenting styles that shaped Marissa and Terrence?

Marissa, with her need for structure and control, likely grew up in an authoritarian home. Her parents may have emphasized order, discipline, and responsibility from a young age. She learned that success meant preparation, planning, and following the rules. Any deviation from that felt like a personal failure, and she carried that mindset into her professional life.

Terrence might have been raised in a permissive environment. His parents probably let him explore his creativity without many boundaries, allowing him to figure things out in his own time. As an adult, this gave him confidence in his spontaneous approach, but it also meant he didn't always appreciate the need for structure or deadlines.

The clash between Marissa and Terrence wasn't just about work styles—it was about their deeply ingrained beliefs about how life should function, beliefs that were formed long before they ever set foot in the office.

TRAUMA-INFORMED COMMUNICATION: THE KEY TO UNDERSTANDING

Imagine how different things could have been if Marissa and Terrence had understood each other's backgrounds. Instead of assuming Terrence was careless, Marissa could have seen his approach as a product of his upbringing. Instead of thinking Marissa was overbearing, Terrence could have understood that her need for control came from a place of fear that if everything wasn't perfect, things would fall apart.

This is where trauma-informed communication comes into play. It's about recognizing that the way we communicate, the way we handle conflict, and the way we navigate relationships are all shaped by our past experiences. When we understand the parenting styles and childhood environments that shaped us, we can begin to communicate with more empathy and less judgment.

For Marissa and Terrence, trauma-informed communication would mean seeing beyond the surface-level frustration and acknowledging the fears and needs driving their behavior. Marissa's anxiety about control wasn't just about the project—it was about her deeply rooted fear of failure. And Terrence's laid-back attitude wasn't about disrespect—it was about his belief that flexibility leads to creativity.

By recognizing these patterns, they could learn to communicate in ways that respected each other's strengths and weaknesses. Instead of clashing, they could find ways to complement each other, Marissa bringing the structure and Terrence bringing the creativity. Trauma-informed communication allows us to see the bigger picture, turning irreconcilable differences into opportunities for growth and connection.

By now, you may be realizing that much of how we communicate, handle conflict, and navigate relationships is deeply influenced by our past, particularly by the way we were parented and the traumatic experiences we might have endured. Adverse childhood experiences (ACEs), as we explored, leave an imprint on how we react in moments of tension, while parenting styles shape our fundamental beliefs about trust, boundaries, and connection. These influences can make what we perceive as irreconcilable differences even more difficult to understand.

But just as trauma can complicate communication, it can also provide the very clues we need to improve it. This is where trauma-informed communication knowledge (TICK) comes into play. TICK is about recognizing how past experiences, especially trauma, influence the way someone communicates, and it's about learning how to approach differences and conversations with empathy and awareness of those deeper wounds.

Many of the challenges we face in relationships stem not from a lack of love but from a lack of understanding of how trauma influences behavior. It's not that we don't care about our partners, family, or friends; it's that we lack the knowledge needed to understand the deeper forces at play in our interactions. When you realize that someone's reaction in a discussion isn't just about what was said in the moment but connected to their past pain, it changes how you approach them. TICK is a method of seeing beyond the surface-level interaction to the underlying emotional triggers.

Let's start with a scenario most of us have gone through: You've had a long day at work, and when you come home, your partner immediately starts telling you about an issue they've been dealing with. Without thinking, you give them advice—after all, you want to help them. But instead of appreciating your input, your partner shuts down, gets quiet, or becomes irritated.

What just happened?

In this moment, your partner wasn't just reacting to the conversation. They were likely reacting from an emotional space shaped by past experiences. Maybe growing up, they had parents who didn't really listen to them, so now they react defensively when they feel unheard. Or maybe they grew up in an environment where expressing needs was discouraged, so being vulnerable feels uncomfortable.

This is where TICK becomes essential. Trauma-informed communication isn't just about what you say, but about how you understand the person you're communicating with.

The same applies in friendships, workplaces, and other relationships. The more you understand the other person's emotional landscape, the more you can adjust your approach to create connection rather than conflict. For example, in a work setting, a colleague might seem overly critical, but through the lens of TICK, you might realize that they've been conditioned to expect failure because of an environment where they were constantly scrutinized. Rather than feeling attacked, you can adjust your response to support and encourage them.

Understanding How Trauma Shapes Reactions

Let's dive deeper into some practical applications of how trauma shows up in communication. These aren't about diagnosing or labeling people but about noticing patterns that help you practice empathy. Let's revisit some of the individuals we've already met in earlier chapters.

The conflict-avoidant partner. Remember Jordan and Taylor? Jordan grew up in a home where conflict was constant and explosive. Whenever his parents fought, Jordan would hide in his room, waiting for the shouting to end. As an adult, Jordan learned that silence and withdrawal were the safest responses to confrontation. Taylor, his partner, grew up in a more expressive household, where conflicts were discussed openly and feelings were aired out until resolution was found.

So when Taylor tries to confront Jordan about an issue in their relationship, Jordan shuts down. No matter how calmly Taylor approaches the subject, Jordan's trauma response kicks in. He becomes distant, physically present but emotionally absent, feeling overwhelmed by the mere idea of conflict.

At this point, Taylor could interpret Jordan's silence as apathy or avoidance. But through TICK, Taylor learns to see this as a trauma response, a survival mechanism Jordan developed in childhood. Armed with this understanding, Taylor can approach the conversation differently: "Jordan, I can see you're feeling overwhelmed right now. I'm not here to attack you—I just want us to talk through this so we can feel closer."

This shifts the dynamic. Instead of pushing harder or feeling rejected, Taylor gives Jordan space, offering reassurance that the conversation is safe and necessary, but it can happen when Jordan is ready.

The perfectionist colleague: Mia and Darrell work together on a high-stakes project. Darrell is detail-oriented and meticulous; he won't let a single thing slip through the cracks. Mia, on the other hand, is a visionary. She focuses on the big picture and doesn't get bogged down in the small stuff.

After one particularly intense meeting, Darrell feels frustrated with Mia's laid-back approach. "Why doesn't she care about the details?" he thinks. "Why isn't she stressing over this deadline like I am?"

Through a TICK lens, Darrell might come to understand that his need for perfection is rooted in childhood experiences where he was praised only when he got everything right. In contrast,

Mia might have grown up in a family where risk-taking and thinking outside the box were encouraged, and "good enough" was celebrated.

Instead of seeing Mia's behavior as laziness, Darrell could reframe his perspective: "Mia approaches things differently because of how she was shaped by her experiences. Her vision complements my attention to detail."

By applying TICK, Darrell can then approach Mia with empathy: "I really value your creative ideas. Let's figure out how we can balance that with the details so we don't miss anything important." This kind of communication allows both their strengths to flourish, rather than causing unnecessary tension.

APPLYING TICK TO SENSITIVE CONVERSATIONS

TICK isn't just about recognizing the trauma, it's about changing the way we respond to it. Here's how you can apply TICK in your own relationships:

Shift from judgment to curiosity. Instead of jumping to conclusions about why someone is behaving a certain way, practice curiosity. Ask yourself, "What might be behind this reaction?" Trauma-informed communication means assuming there's more beneath the surface than meets the eye.

Example: If your partner is quick to anger, instead of thinking, "They're always so reactive," ask, "What might be triggering this? Are they feeling threatened or insecure?"

Create emotional safety. Trauma often causes people to feel unsafe in vulnerable moments. Your goal is to create a space where it's okay to share feelings without fear of judgment or retaliation. This doesn't mean avoiding difficult conversations, but it does mean approaching them with compassion.

Example: Instead of escalating an argument, you might say, "I can see that this is a sensitive topic. Let's talk about it when we both feel calmer."

Use trauma-informed language. Pay attention to the words you use during difficult conversations. Avoid language that triggers defensiveness, and instead, use words that promote understanding and empathy.

Example: Instead of saying, "You never listen to me," try, "I feel unheard when we have these conversations. Can we try to find a way where we both feel understood?"

Recognize emotional triggers. Everyone has emotional triggers that are linked to their past experiences. TICK encourages you to recognize these triggers in both yourself and others, allowing you to de-escalate situations before they spiral.

Example: If you know your partner gets triggered when discussing money because they grew up in a financially unstable home, approach the topic with extra sensitivity. Instead of saying, "We need to talk about our budget now," try, "I know money can be a stressful subject. Let's work through this together at a time when we're both ready."

TICK as a Tool for Compassion

Trauma-informed communication knowledge isn't about walking on eggshells or avoiding conflict, it's about shifting how we approach difficult conversations. It allows us to see beyond the surface behaviors, tapping into the deeper emotional landscape shaped by past experiences.

TICK helps us approach our relationships with curiosity, compassion, and communication rather than reacting from a place of frustration or confusion. By acknowledging the trauma that shapes us, we give ourselves and others the grace to heal and grow.

As we transition to the next chapter, we'll take this understanding even deeper by exploring attachment styles—the lasting impact that early relationships with our caregivers has on the way we approach intimacy, trust, and connection in adulthood. These insights will further equip us to use TICK in a way that promotes meaningful, lasting transformation in our relationships.

PONDER POINTS

1. Which parenting style most closely resembles the environment you grew up in, and how might that still shape your responses in adult relationships?

2. How do you typically respond in moments of stress or conflict: Do you lean toward control, avoidance, or connection? Why do you think that is?

3. In what ways can you begin using TICK (trauma-informed communication knowledge) to better understand and respond to the emotional needs of those around you?

PRAYER

Lord, help me see beyond the surface of my reactions and the reactions of others. Give me wisdom to understand the roots beneath the tension and grace to respond with compassion, not judgment. Heal the places in me that still operate from fear, and teach me how to love with clarity, courage, and care. Amen.

9

WHY WE REACH, WHY WE RUN

Attachment Styles and the Dance of Connection

HAVE YOU EVER WONDERED WHY SOME PEOPLE seem to effortlessly navigate relationships, while others struggle with feelings of insecurity or emotional distance? It's not just personality or circumstance at play—much of it comes down to attachment styles, a concept that may be new to many. Simply put, attachment styles describe the patterns we develop in how we connect to and depend on others. These patterns begin in childhood, based on our early experiences with caregivers, and carry through into adulthood, shaping the way we relate to partners, friends, and even coworkers.

Your attachment style is like a blueprint for how you love, trust, and respond to intimacy. Whether you tend to feel secure in relationships or struggle with fear of abandonment, or whether you seek closeness or avoid it, these tendencies are often rooted in the attachment patterns you developed in your earliest years. And as we dive deeper into this chapter, we explore how adverse childhood experiences (ACEs) and parenting styles intersect with these attachment styles to create unique relational dynamics. By understanding these patterns, you can gain insight into your own behavior and that of those around you, opening the door to deeper connections and healthier relationships.

Understanding attachment styles gives us the language to describe the invisible forces that drive how we interact with those we love. These styles are not just habits or preferences; they are deeply ingrained ways of responding to emotional closeness and vulnerability. While these patterns begin with our caregivers, they show up in our adult relationships—whether it's in marriage, friendships, or even professional settings.

In essence, attachment styles are the key to unlocking why we respond to intimacy the way we do, and more importantly, they offer us the opportunity to change. But, as we've explored throughout this book, our early experiences—our ACEs, the way we were parented, and the trauma we carry with us—shape these attachment styles, for better or for worse.

THE FOUR MAIN ATTACHMENT STYLES

There are four primary attachment styles: secure, anxious, avoidant, and fearful-avoidant (disorganized). Each style reveals a unique way of approaching love and relationships, and by identifying our own style—and the style of those we are in relationships with—we can learn to communicate better, heal old wounds, and, ultimately, move toward deeper connection.

Secure. A secure attachment style creates a foundation of trust and stability. This form of attachment is formed in an environment where caregivers are consistently responsive, nurturing, and attuned to the child's emotional needs. This type of parenting involves clear communication, warmth, and appropriate boundaries. Parents of securely attached children are not perfect, but they are dependable. They provide a safe space for the child to explore their emotions, make mistakes, and grow, all while knowing they will be supported and understood.

Imagine a young boy who scrapes his knee while playing outside. He runs to his father, crying in pain. Instead of brushing off his tears or telling him to "be tough," his father kneels down to his level, embraces him, and says, "I see that hurt you. It's okay, son." He gently cleans his wound, all the while offering words of comfort and assurance. The boy feels seen and understood, and he knows he can rely on his father for comfort and understanding when things go wrong.

After the boy has calmed down, his father encourages him to return to play. He's not overprotective but offers his son the confidence to re-engage with the world, knowing he's secure in his love and support. Over time, these types of interactions teach the boy that relationships are safe, that people can be trusted, and that his emotions are valid.

This type of caregiving fosters a secure attachment because it balances love and independence. The boy grows up understanding that while his parents will always be there when he needs them, he is also capable of handling challenges on his own. As an adult, the young man carries this confidence into his relationships; he is able to give and receive love without fear of abandonment or rejection. He knows how to express his needs and trusts that his partner will be there to support him.

Anxious. Let's move to the anxious attachment style, which is formed in a more unpredictable environment. This style develops when caregivers are inconsistent in their responsiveness— sometimes they're available and nurturing, and other times they may be distant or preoccupied. This inconsistency creates confusion for the child, who never knows when their emotional needs will be met. As a result, they become hyper-attuned to their caregiver's moods and behaviors, always seeking reassurance but never feeling fully secure.

Picture a young girl named Maddie. Maddie's mother is loving and attentive when she's in a good mood, but when work is stressful or personal challenges arise, her mother withdraws emotionally. One day Maddie falls off her bike and runs to her mother for comfort. Her mother, dealing with a difficult phone call, responds with irritation: "Not now, Maddie. You're fine." Maddie is left feeling confused and alone, wondering what she did wrong and why her mother, who is sometimes so loving, is now so distant.

On a different day, when Maddie brings home a drawing from school, her mother enthusiastically praises her. "You're so talented! This is beautiful, Maddie!" The warmth and affection fill Maddie with happiness. But she doesn't know when this warmth will be replaced by coldness again, so she clings to these moments of affection, desperate for more validation.

As Maddie grows, this emotional uncertainty becomes the foundation of her anxious attachment style. She becomes highly sensitive to any perceived distance in her relationships, constantly seeking reassurance from friends and partners. In her adult relationships, Maddie may overanalyze her partner's behavior, interpreting small actions—like a delayed text or a quiet mood—as signs that he's losing interest or preparing to leave. This fear of abandonment can lead to clinginess or emotional volatility, driven by a deep-seated anxiety that love is always at risk of being withdrawn.

While Maddie's need for closeness is genuine, her anxiety prevents her from fully trusting the security of her relationships, leaving her in a constant state of emotional vigilance. Understanding this anxious attachment pattern is key to healing, as it allows people like Maddie to recognize that the inconsistency of their early caregiving doesn't have to dictate the emotional landscape of their future relationships.

Avoidant. On the other hand, an avoidant attachment style develops when caregivers are emotionally distant or dismissive. In this environment, a child learns early on that expressing their emotions is either discouraged or ignored, leading them to suppress their feelings in order to cope. The message they receive is that relying on others is futile, and the only person they can depend on is themselves. This self-reliance becomes a defense mechanism, designed to protect them from the pain of rejection or neglect.

For example, let's look back at Marcus. Growing up, Marcus was a boy whose parents were well-meaning but emotionally unavailable. His father worked long hours, and when he was home, he expected silence and order. His mother, overwhelmed with her own stresses, offered minimal emotional support. When Marcus tried to talk about how he felt, he was often met with responses like, "Don't make a big deal out of it," or "You need to toughen up." Over time, Marcus stopped sharing his feelings altogether. He internalized the belief that showing vulnerability would only lead to disappointment, so he built emotional walls to protect himself.

One day, Marcus comes home from school after being bullied. His instinct is to retreat to his room, hiding the pain he feels inside. His parents don't notice anything is wrong, and Marcus doesn't seek their comfort—he has learned that he must deal with it on his own. This withdrawal from emotional connection is the beginning of an avoidant attachment style.

As Marcus grows into adulthood, these emotional walls remain firmly in place. In his relationships, Marcus is seen as distant. When his partner, Tasha, expresses her desire for more emotional intimacy, Marcus feels overwhelmed and suffocated. He withdraws, either by physically leaving the room or emotionally shutting down. He doesn't do this out of malice but because he's learned that getting too close can lead to vulnerability, and vulnerability leads to pain.

For Marcus, closeness feels like a threat to his independence, and he may struggle to stay present during emotional conversations. His need for distance isn't a reflection of how he feels about his partner, but rather a deeply ingrained protective mechanism. Understanding his avoidant attachment style helps Marcus and others like him realize that emotional closeness doesn't have to be dangerous. Healing can begin when avoidantly attached individuals learn it's okay to lean on others and intimacy doesn't mean losing oneself.

Fearful-avoidant. Finally, let's look at the fearful-avoidant (disorganized) attachment style, which is the most complex of the four. This style often develops in children who experience a chaotic or abusive home environment, where their caregivers are a source of both comfort and fear. Children with this attachment style face a confusing emotional dilemma: they crave closeness but are simultaneously terrified of it. This push-pull dynamic makes relationships feel unpredictable and frightening. As these children grow up, they carry a deeply ingrained sense of unpredictability into their adult relationships. On one hand, they long for intimacy and connection; on the other hand, they are terrified that this closeness will bring pain or rejection. This results in a cycle of emotional whiplash, where they oscillate between seeking closeness and pushing it away.

Let's dive deeper into Marcus's story. If his parents weren't just emotionally distant but also unpredictable—sometimes affectionate and supportive, at other times angry or neglectful—he would learn to associate love with fear and inconsistency. He may crave affection but not trust that it will last, always bracing himself for the emotional rug to be pulled out from under him.

In Marcus's adult relationships, this manifests as fearful-avoidant attachment. When he first meets Tasha, he's drawn to the idea of closeness and connection. He may even be highly affectionate in the early stages of their relationship. But as soon as things start to deepen, Marcus begins to feel vulnerable. He recalls, often subconsciously, how his parents' love was conditional or fleeting. This creates an internal conflict: He wants to be close to Tasha but feels that opening up fully might lead to rejection or disappointment, just as it did with his parents.

For instance, Marcus might plan a romantic evening with Tasha, fully intending to deepen their connection. But halfway through, something she says triggers a memory from his childhood, a subtle reminder of when love felt unsafe. Without even realizing it, Marcus begins to withdraw. He becomes emotionally distant, perhaps making a sarcastic comment or changing the subject to something trivial. Tasha, confused by this sudden shift, tries to engage with him, but Marcus feels overwhelmed and shuts down completely, leaving her feeling hurt and rejected.

This emotional push-pull leaves both partners feeling trapped in a cycle of confusion. For Marcus, the closeness he desires feels just out of reach, while Tasha can't understand why Marcus seems to want connection but consistently pulls away when it's within their grasp.

The fearful-avoidant attachment style creates a deep-seated fear of abandonment paired with an equally strong fear of intimacy. Individuals with this style often feel stuck in limbo, unable to fully trust their partner yet unable to let go of the relationship. They may vacillate between craving closeness and erecting walls when the relationship starts to feel too real.

Understanding this attachment style is crucial for both individuals in the relationship. For Marcus, recognizing that his behaviors stem from childhood trauma, and not from a lack of love for Tasha, can help him begin the process of healing. For Tasha, learning to interpret Marcus's withdrawal as a sign of fear rather than disinterest can help her approach their conflicts with more compassion.

Ultimately, the fearful-avoidant attachment style can be navigated, but it requires patience, self-awareness, and a willingness to unpack the layers of fear and trauma that have shaped these responses. By learning to communicate openly and by seeking professional support if necessary, individuals with fearful-avoidant attachment can begin to build healthier, more secure relationships, where closeness is no longer synonymous with fear.

Identifying attachment styles in yourself or in others is key to understanding the underlying dynamics of your relationships. The good news is that by paying close attention to patterns of behavior—both your own and those of the people around you—you can begin to recognize which attachment style might be at play. Let's explore how you can identify each attachment style in yourself and in your partner, friend, or coworker, while keeping in mind that many behaviors stem from deeper emotional patterns learned in childhood.

Identifying Secure Attachment

For yourself:

- Do you generally feel comfortable expressing your emotions and needs in relationships?

- Are you able to trust your partner or friends without feeling overly anxious about losing them?

- When conflicts arise, do you feel confident in your ability to work through them without fearing that the relationship will fall apart?

- Are you able to maintain a healthy balance between independence and connection?

If you find that you answer "yes" to these questions, you may have a secure attachment style. Securely attached individuals are generally comfortable with emotional intimacy and trust others easily, allowing them to form stable, long-lasting relationships. They are also comfortable with their own space and their partner's, without feeling neglected or abandoned.

In your partner, friend, or coworker:

- Do they seem open and responsive to your needs without being overly dependent or distant?

- Are they reliable when it comes to communication, and do they handle conflicts without becoming excessively defensive or detached?

- Do they express care and affection consistently, without hot-and-cold behavior?

A partner or coworker with a secure attachment style will be approachable and dependable. They are good at balancing their

needs with the needs of the relationship, and they handle disagreements with maturity and empathy.

IDENTIFYING ANXIOUS ATTACHMENT

For yourself:

- Do you often find yourself feeling anxious or insecure in
  relationships, fearing that the other person may
  abandon you?

- Do you crave constant reassurance from your partner or
  friends to feel secure?

- When there's a conflict, do you immediately assume the
  worst and worry that the relationship is in jeopardy?

- Are you often preoccupied with thoughts of the other
  person, checking in frequently or feeling upset if they don't
  respond right away?

If you identify with these behaviors, you may have an anxious
attachment style. People with this attachment style often feel that
they need to be in constant contact with their partner or loved
ones to feel secure, and they can become easily distressed when
things don't go according to plan.

In your partner, friend, or coworker:

- Do they frequently ask for reassurance, even when things
  are going well?

- Do they have a tendency to overthink conflicts or read into
  small behaviors, such as a delayed text response, as signs of
  trouble in the relationship?

- Do they often feel neglected or unloved, even when you've
  done your best to meet their needs?

Someone with an anxious attachment style may seem overly concerned with the status of the relationship. They may check in frequently, ask for reassurance, or react strongly to small signs of perceived rejection.

IDENTIFYING AVOIDANT ATTACHMENT

For yourself:

- Do you prefer to handle things on your own, without relying on others for emotional support?

- Do you find it difficult to open up to others or express your feelings, even with those you're closest to?

- When conflict arises, do you tend to withdraw or shut down emotionally rather than engage in the conversation?

- Do you value independence above all else, sometimes feeling like relationships require too much emotional involvement?

If this sounds like you, you may have an avoidant attachment style. Avoidantly attached individuals are uncomfortable with too much closeness and tend to distance themselves emotionally to protect themselves from getting hurt. They often feel like relying on others makes them vulnerable, so they avoid it.

In your partner, friend, or coworker:

- Do they tend to pull away or become distant when things get emotionally intense?

- Do they avoid discussing feelings or personal topics, preferring to keep things surface-level?

- Are they highly self-reliant, sometimes to the point of seeming detached or uninterested in deepening the relationship?

A person with an avoidant attachment style will often retreat when things get emotionally challenging. They value their independence and may avoid vulnerability because it feels too risky or uncomfortable.

IDENTIFYING FEARFUL-AVOIDANT (DISORGANIZED) ATTACHMENT

For yourself:

- Do you experience a push-pull dynamic in relationships, where you crave closeness but also fear it?

- Do you often feel overwhelmed by intimacy and then withdraw, even though you want a deep connection?

- Do you find that your relationships are marked by a cycle of emotional highs and lows, with feelings of insecurity surfacing unexpectedly?

- Do you feel as though you can't trust others fully, even when they're trying to support you?

If you resonate with these behaviors, you might have a fearful-avoidant attachment style. People with this style often feel torn between their desire for intimacy and their deep-seated fear that being too close will lead to hurt. This creates a confusing dynamic where they may become close to someone emotionally, only to pull away when the connection becomes too intense.

In your partner, friend, or coworker:

- Do they sometimes seem intensely interested in the relationship, only to pull back suddenly when things start getting serious?

- Do they express a deep need for love and connection, but also exhibit behaviors that create emotional distance?

- Are their responses to conflict or emotional closeness unpredictable, alternating between neediness and withdrawal?

People with fearful-avoidant attachment often experience their relationships as a confusing mix of longing and fear. They may seem enthusiastic about deepening the connection one day but become distant or even cold the next.

USING TICK (TRAUMA-INFORMED COMMUNICATION KNOWLEDGE)

Now that you've identified these attachment styles, you can use the concept of TICK to communicate more effectively. Trauma-informed communication isn't about excusing behavior, but about recognizing that each person's way of relating to others has deep roots in their past experiences.

For someone with a secure attachment style, open and honest communication is usually enough to maintain a strong relationship. They appreciate straightforwardness and consistency, so continue to be reliable and clear in your interactions.

For someone with an anxious attachment style, it's important to offer reassurance. Acknowledge their feelings and make an effort to be responsive when they reach out, even if it's just to say, "I hear you, and I'm here for you." Avoid dismissing their concerns, as this can trigger their anxiety.

For someone with an avoidant attachment style, try giving them the space they need while gently encouraging emotional openness over time. Let them know that you value their independence, but that you're also there if and when they're ready to talk. Avoid pushing them into emotionally intense situations too quickly.

For someone with a fearful-avoidant attachment style, it's key to create a safe environment where they feel both supported and free to express their fears. Recognize their internal conflict and offer steady reassurance that it's okay to feel vulnerable. Avoid sudden emotional demands, and instead, allow the relationship to develop at a pace that feels safe for both of you.

PONDER POINTS

1. Which attachment style do you most identify with, and how do you see it showing up in your closest relationships? Reflect not only on your romantic or family relationships, but also how you respond to trust, conflict, and emotional need.

2. What messages did your caregivers, through their actions or inaction, teach you about love, safety, and dependence? How might those early lessons still be influencing your ability to connect today?

3. Where do you sense God inviting you into a more secure form of connection—with him, with yourself, and with others?

4. What might healing look like if your sense of worth was rooted in being fully seen and loved by God?

PRAYER

Father, you are the One who formed me for relationship, first with you, then with others. Heal the parts of me shaped by fear, rejection, or inconsistency. Teach me how to receive love without anxiety and give love without retreat. Restore my blueprint of connection to reflect your faithfulness, and lead me into healthier, more secure relationships. I trust that what was broken can be rebuilt in your grace. Amen.

10

MAKING IT WORK

Tools for Real-Life Connection

As we transition from understanding attachment styles to applying real-world strategies, it becomes clear that connecting across differences isn't just about understanding our differences, it's about how we respond to them. We've delved into the roots of our emotional and relational dynamics, from childhood trauma and parenting styles to attachment patterns. But the question now becomes: how do we move from knowing these things to applying them in a way that heals and strengthens our relationships?

Throughout the Bible, we're called to live and move with empathy and grace, but also with knowledge, wisdom, and understanding. Proverbs 4:7 reminds us, "Wisdom is the principal thing; therefore get wisdom: and with all thy getting get understanding." This is not just an intellectual pursuit but a relational one. The key to navigating relational challenges isn't merely knowing about them; it's understanding how to bridge the emotional and spiritual gaps they create.

Take a moment to reflect on your own life. Perhaps you've found yourself in a situation where you just couldn't understand why your partner, friend, or even colleague reacted in certain ways.

You tried to communicate, but every time you did, it felt like you were speaking two different languages. This isn't a lack of love or effort; it's often a lack of understanding. It's where many relationships falter—caught between love and frustration simply because we don't have the tools to communicate in ways that create connection instead of conflict.

Colossians 3:13-14 reminds us of the path forward: "Forbearing one another, and forgiving one another, if any man have a quarrel against any: even as Christ forgave you, so also do ye. And above all these things put on charity, which is the bond of perfectness." Reconciliation isn't always about eliminating differences, it's about learning to live with them in a way that honors God and deepens our connection with others.

LIVING OUT THE MINISTRY OF RECONNECTION

Let's take trauma-informed communication as a foundational example. Understanding how trauma shapes behavior allows us to approach our relationships with greater empathy. When someone withdraws or becomes defensive, we may be tempted to react with frustration or judgment. But with a trauma-informed perspective, we can pause and ask, "What pain might be causing this reaction?" This is exactly how Jesus approached people in need: He saw beyond their actions and understood their hearts.

Remember the woman at the well in John 4? Jesus didn't just see her past; he saw her thirst for connection. Instead of leading with judgment, he led with truth wrapped in grace. In the same way, we're called to recognize the pain behind the behavior, allowing compassion to guide our response.

Consider a situation where your partner seems distant after an argument. Without understanding, this could easily escalate. But when you recognize that their distance may be connected to an avoidant attachment style or a history of emotional neglect, your response changes. Instead of demanding closeness on your terms, you give them space while offering gentle assurance. This becomes a bridge-building moment, one where wisdom, grace, and timing create the possibility for healing.

REPAIR ATTEMPTS: SMALL BRIDGES THAT SAVE BIG RELATIONSHIPS

Another practical strategy for relational connection is found in the repair attempts and emotional bids we discussed in chapter five. These small gestures—like offering a kind word during an argument or acknowledging the other person's feelings—are much more than just conflict-resolution tools. They're acts of biblical grace. In Romans 12:18, Paul instructs us, "If it be possible, as much as lieth in you, live peaceably with all men." Repair attempts create that peace by signaling, "I care about you more than this argument."

These are not just marital strategies, they're life skills for any meaningful relationship. A text to check in with a sibling after a disagreement, a soft tone during a tense meeting, or an honest "I was wrong" are all relational olive branches. They don't erase the conflict, but they create room for repair.

THE POWER OF EVERYDAY EMPATHY

Bridge-building isn't limited to moments of conflict. It's about cultivating empathy as a daily habit. The Bible calls us to "rejoice with them that do rejoice, and weep with them that weep" (Romans 12:15). Empathy is a spiritual discipline. It requires us to leave the safety of our own assumptions and step into the world of another, if only for a moment.

Let's return to Marcus and Tasha. Their relationship was full of emotional triggers. Marcus's avoidant tendencies often made Tasha feel ignored, while her anxious style led her to seek constant reassurance. The turning point in their journey wasn't a big conversation; it was a series of small, empathic shifts. Marcus began to recognize that Tasha's questions weren't criticisms; they were emotional bids. Tasha began to realize that Marcus's silence wasn't rejection—it was fear.

This kind of mutual empathy changed their relationship. It didn't erase their differences, but it made space for understanding. And in that space, love grew.

BIBLICAL BRIDGE-BUILDING PRACTICES

So how do we build these bridges in practical, biblical ways?

Speak the truth in love. Ephesians 4:15 tells us to speak "the truth in love." That means we don't have to abandon honesty—but we do need to deliver it with grace. Before correcting someone, ask yourself: Is this helpful? Is this loving? Is now the right time?

Listen to understand, not to defend. James 1:19 gives us this timeless wisdom: "Let every man be swift to hear, slow to speak, slow to wrath." Listening with humility creates a path for real communication. Often people don't need us to fix their problem; they just want to feel heard.

Respond, don't react. Proverbs 15:1 says, "A soft answer turneth away wrath: but grievous words stir up anger." When you feel triggered, take a breath. Ask yourself what response would de-escalate the moment and invite connection rather than defensiveness.

Practice self-awareness and repentance. Matthew 7:5 challenges us, "First cast out the beam out of thine own eye." Part of building bridges is being willing to examine your own patterns. Are you approaching conversations from a place of fear, pride, or wound-edness? Invite God into that process of reflection and repentance.

Prioritize peace over power. Romans 14:19 encourages us to "follow after the things which make for peace." That doesn't mean avoiding hard conversations, but it means valuing unity over the need to be right.

YOU'RE NOT ALONE IN THE WORK

Finally, remember: you don't have to do this alone. Relationships are spiritual terrain, and God promises to guide us through them. Isaiah 58:11 assures us, "And the LORD shall guide thee continually, and satisfy thy soul in drought, and make fat thy bones: and thou shalt be like a watered garden." When you're exhausted, when the bridge seems too long or broken, God meets you there.

You are not expected to love others perfectly. You are simply invited to show up—with truth, with humility, and with a will-ingness to build one brick at a time. Each choice to listen, to pause, to offer grace is a holy act of construction, a bridge rising between two hearts.

As we reach this final chapter of our journey together, I want to take a moment to speak directly to you. You've walked with me through the complexities of trauma, parenting styles, attachment patterns, and the nuances of communication. You've explored the depths of your own story and, perhaps, begun to see your relation-ships with new eyes. Now I want to share one last truth with you—a truth that has shaped the entire message of this book: your differences are not a mistake.

I know that in our culture, differences are often seen as a hin-derance. In fact, in divorce we use the phrase "irreconcilable differences" when we feel like we've exhausted every option. When we've tried to make things work and it seems like we're just too different to find common ground. But remember those very differences—the ones that feel like barriers—are actually invita- tions. Invitations to grow, to change, and to transform, both within yourself and in your relationships. Differences are not the con- tention of relationships, they are the beginning of transformation and deeper connection.

The Bible tells us in Romans 12:2, "Be not conformed to this world: but be ye transformed by the renewing of your mind." What if the pattern of this world—the belief that differences are insurmountable—could be broken? What if instead of running from our differences, we saw them as part of the divine blueprint God laid out for each of us?

Let's be honest. This journey hasn't been easy. We've delved into some deep waters, exploring how adverse childhood expe- riences (ACEs) leave lasting imprints on our souls, how par- enting styles shape us more than we often realize, and how attachment patterns play out in our relationships. But all of this has led us here—to this moment of clarity. God never intended for us to avoid the tension. We are called to walk through it, to grow from it, and to become more like God in the process.

I won't sugarcoat it. Transformation is uncomfortable. It's messy. It often requires us to look in the mirror and confront parts of ourselves we'd rather not see. But here's the thing: God isn't afraid of our mess. In fact, God invites us to bring our mess to him, to allow him to do the work of refining us. And that work often begins in the places where we feel the most tension, the places where our differences seem irreconcilable.

Think back to some of the examples we've discussed—whether it was Marcus struggling with avoidant attachment or the colleagues at work who couldn't seem to see eye to eye. In each case, the tension wasn't the enemy. The differences weren't the problem. The problem was how they were approaching the tension. When we view our differences as obstacles, we shut down. We withdraw, we become defensive, we stonewall. But when we begin to see those differences as part of God's design—as tools he uses to shape us—everything changes.

Here's a truth I've come to learn, both in my own life and in the countless relationships I've coached: God's purpose is not for us to run from differences but to lean into them with grace, empathy, and wisdom. Why? Because differences are where growth happens. They're where love deepens. They're where we learn to die to ourselves and live for the greater good of the relationship.

Throughout this book, we've explored the "why" behind many of the behaviors that challenge us in relationships. We've learned that trauma, attachment styles, and our upbringing all shape how we show up in the world. But knowing isn't enough. What do we do with that knowledge? How do we apply it when the rubber meets the road?

The Bible calls us to live with grace, "forbearing one another, and forgiving one another, if any man have a quarrel against any: even as Christ forgave you, so also do ye" (Colossians 3:13). Grace doesn't ignore the hurt. It doesn't sweep differences under the rug. But it makes space for healing. It creates room for us to say, "I see where you're coming from. I don't fully understand it, but I'm willing to listen. I'm willing to meet you halfway."

And this is where understanding comes into play. Empathy is the key to unlocking the door to deeper connection. But empathy can flourish only when we seek first to understand. Understanding requires us to set aside our assumptions, our defensiveness, and our need to be right. It asks us to step into the other person's shoes, to see the world from their perspective, and to respond with compassion.

When we choose to embrace the differences in our relationships —when we stop seeing them as obstacles and start seeing them as opportunities for growth—something beautiful happens. We begin to reflect the very image of God in a way that is more complete, more whole. The Bible says we are all made in God's image, yet we know that no single person reflects the fullness of who God is. It's in our diversity that we find the true reflection of God's character.

Your partner's need for structure and order? That's a reflection of God's wisdom and precision. Your friend's creativity and spontaneity? That's a reflection of God's boundless creativity. Your child's desire for independence? That's a reflection of God's freedom. When we embrace our differences, we begin to see the many facets of God's character displayed in those around us.

And this is what irreconcilable differences are truly about. They aren't about division, they're about revelation. They reveal the fullness of God's character in ways we could never see if we all thought, acted, and felt the same. They call us to a higher level of understanding, to a deeper well of grace, and to a more profound experience of love.

So where do we go from here? How do we move forward when we've spent years fighting against the very differences God designed to enrich our lives?

We start by surrendering. Surrender the need to have it all figured out. Surrender the need to be right. Surrender the belief that your way is the only way. And in that place of surrender, invite God to show you how to move with grace, empathy, understanding, and celebration.

Next, we practice what we've learned. Whether it's the "yes, and" technique, trauma-informed communication knowledge (TICK), or understanding the power of attachment styles, we take these tools and apply them in our everyday interactions. We practice humility when we're faced with tension. We offer grace when we feel hurt. We seek understanding when we're tempted to judge.

And finally, we commit to the process of transformation. Relationships don't change overnight. They grow, evolve, and deepen over time. But the good news is that we don't walk this path alone. God is with us every step of the way, guiding us, equipping us, and giving us the strength to navigate even the most irreconcilable of differences.

As we close this chapter, I want to leave you with this: The journey you're on is sacred. The differences you encounter in your relationships are not random, they are part of the divine blueprint God has laid out for your life. And while the road may be challenging, it is also filled with opportunities to grow, to learn, to love more deeply, and to reflect the image of God in ways you never thought possible.

So as you move forward, remember this: God doesn't call us to avoid our differences, he calls us to embrace them. And in doing so, we discover more not only about the people in our lives but about the God who created us all.

Thank you for walking this journey with me. I pray that this book has been more than just a guide but a companion, a source of hope and encouragement, and a reminder that your irreconcilable differences were intentionally designed by God and are a gift—both to you and to those around you.

PONDER POINTS

1. What if your greatest relational challenges aren't meant to break you, but to build you?

2. Instead of resisting the tension, ask: What is God trying to form in me through this difference?

3. Healing doesn't come from avoiding hard conversations; it comes from entering them with wisdom, grace, and empathy.

4. What would shift in your relationships if you prioritized understanding over being right?

5. You don't have to fix everything to walk in love.

6. Sometimes the most transformative thing you can offer is presence, patience, and a willingness to try again.

PRAYER

Lord, help me to stop running from the differences that challenge me and start seeing them as opportunities for transformation. Teach me to love with empathy, to respond with grace, and to build bridges where there once were walls. Make me a peacemaker in a divided world, and let your love guide every step of the journey. Amen.

ACKNOWLEDGMENTS

THIS BOOK WOULD not have been possible without the love, support, and encouragement of those who have walked this journey with me.

To my beautiful wife, Dominque—your unwavering support, deep wisdom, and quiet strength have sustained me through every chapter of this work, both literally and figuratively. You are the love that anchors my purpose.

To my children, Jasmine, Emmanuel, and Joshua, and my bonus daughter Thanh—you are each a daily reminder of God's creativity, grace, and call to legacy. Watching you grow has taught me more about relationships than any research ever could.

To the entire team at Circle Urban Ministries—thank you for being a living example of what it means to build community across differences. Your work, your heart, and your commitment inspire me every single day. I'm especially grateful to our staff and leadership, who walk beside me in the mission of transformation and justice.

To my siblings, Joseph, Mike, and Dr. Millicent Borishade—thank you for your love, laughter, and deep-rooted connection. We share not just history but purpose, and I'm grateful to walk this life with you.

To my niece, Dr. Howell—your brilliance and integrity make our family proud, and your encouragement means more than you know.

To my dear friends, the Stephens family—your presence, prayers, and partnership have been a source of steady encouragement on this journey.

And to the Iron Men, my accountability partners and brothers in Christ—thank you for sharpening me, challenging me, and holding me up. Your honesty and faithfulness have helped me become the man, leader, and author I am today.

Above all, I give glory to God—for entrusting me with this message and calling me to walk the often uncomfortable, yet redemptive, road of reconciliation. May these pages serve as bridges toward deeper understanding, healing, and love.

RECOMMENDED RESOURCES

Books

The books recommended in this section have been carefully selected to deepen your understanding of the topics explored in *Connecting Across Differences*. Whether you're interested in healing from past trauma, improving your communication patterns, or learning more about attachment styles and relational dynamics, these titles offer wisdom, research, and practical tools. Some are grounded in psychological theory, others offer faith-based insight, and many bridge both worlds. I've included books that shaped my thinking and helped countless clients, friends, and readers move toward more secure, meaningful relationships. Consider these not just as background reading but as companions on your journey toward deeper connection.

Kevin Chapman, *Mastering Our Emotions: Biblical Principles for Emotional Health* (InterVarsity Press, 2025). This book integrates clinical psychology with biblical truth to help believers understand and regulate their emotions in a spiritually grounded way. Dr. Kevin Chapman, a licensed psychologist, offers practical tools for managing fear, anger, and sadness while anchoring emotional health in Scripture.

Duane Elmer, *Cross-Cultural Connections: Stepping Out and Fitting In Around the World* (InterVarsity Press, 2002). Ideal for those looking to build bridges across cultural divides, this book provides practical insights into effective crosscultural communication. It's a valuable resource for anyone seeking to understand and connect with people from different backgrounds.

Tim Muehlhoff, *I Beg to Differ: Navigating Difficult Conversations with Truth and Love* (InterVarsity Press, 2014). This book offers strategies for engaging in tough conversations without compromising on truth or love. It's particularly helpful for those seeking to maintain relationships amid disagreements.

Tim Muehlhoff and Todd Lewis, *Authentic Communication: Christian Speech Engaging Culture* (InterVarsity Press, 2010). This book explores how Christians can engage in meaningful and respectful conversations in a diverse culture. It offers guidance on navigating complex communication challenges with grace and truth.

Pete Scazzero, *Emotionally Healthy Spirituality: It's Impossible to Be Spiritually Mature While Remaining Emotionally Immature,* updated ed. (Zondervan, 2017). Pete Scazzero offers a transformative framework for integrating emotional health with spiritual formation. Drawing from his personal journey as a pastor, Scazzero reveals how unresolved emotional wounds can hinder genuine discipleship.

PERSONAL AND RELATIONAL GROWTH ASSESSMENTS

Tom Rath, *StrengthsFinder 2.0* (Gallup, 2007). This system helps you identify your top five strengths and understand how to apply them in work, life, and relationships. See gallup.com/cliftonstrengths.

DiSC Personality Assessment. Available from multiple organizations, DiSC is a practical tool for understanding behavior styles and improving communication with others. See discprofile.com.

Myers-Briggs Type Indicator (MBTI). This personality profiling system explores how individuals perceive the world and make decisions. Useful for understanding relational dynamics. See 16personalities.com (free version).

The Enneagram. A spiritual and psychological tool that reveals your core motivations and defense mechanisms. I recommend Ian Morgan Cron and Suzanne Stabile, *The Road Back to You: An Enneagram Journey to Self-Discovery* (InterVarsity Press, 2016).

Adverse Childhood Experiences (ACEs) Questionnaire. A validated tool for reflecting on early experiences and understanding their potential impact on adult relationships. Visit cdc.gov/violenceprevention/aces.

PRACTICAL RELATIONSHIP TOOLS

The Gottman Card Decks App (The Gottman Institute). Offers research-based prompts for couples, including emotional bids, conflict repair, and connection exercises.

Emotion Wheel. A simple but effective tool for identifying and naming emotions. Especially helpful in conversations involving emotional regulation.

TICK Journal Template. A journaling format designed to apply trauma-informed communication knowledge (TICK). Track emotional triggers, communication patterns, and moments of growth in your relationships.

SPIRITUAL FORMATION AND EMOTIONAL HEALTH

Richard Plass and James Cofield, *The Relational Soul: Moving from False Self to Deep Connection* (InterVarsity Press, 2014). Examines how our relationship with God and others is shaped by early experiences and spiritual formation.

Pete and Geri Scazzero, *Emotionally Healthy Relationships: Discipleship that Deeply Changes Your Relationship with Others*, updated ed. (HarperChristian Resources, 2022). A faith-based framework for developing mature, emotionally intelligent relationships grounded in biblical principles.

Henry Cloud and John Townsend, *Boundaries: When to Say Yes, How to Say No To Take Control of Your Life*, updated and expanded ed. (Zondervan, 2017). A foundational book on establishing healthy boundaries in relationships, work, and ministry.

NOTES

INTRODUCTION

[1]Lucy Peppiatt, *The Imago Dei: Humanity Made in the Image of God* (Cascade Books, 2022).

1. WHAT IF THERE'S NOTHING WRONG WITH YOU?

[1]Tom Rath, *StrengthsFinder 2.0* (Gallup Press, 2007).

2. DESIGNED TO BE DIFFERENT: A LOOK AT CREATION

[1]J. Richard Middleton, *The Liberating Image: The Imago Dei in Genesis 1* (Brazos Press, 2005); John H. Walton, *The Lost World of Genesis One* (InterVarsity Press, 2009).

[2]Richard J. Clifford, *Creation Accounts in the Ancient Near East and in the Bible*, Catholic Biblical Quarterly Monograph Series 26 (Catholic Biblical Association of America, 1994); John H. Walton, *The Lost World of Adam and Eve* (IVP Academic, 2015), 55; The NIV Application Commentary (Zondervan, 2001).

[3]Phyllis Trible, *God and the Rhetoric of Sexuality* (Fortress Press, 1978).

[4]Nahum M. Sarna, *Genesis: The Traditional Hebrew Text with New JPS Translation*, The JPS Torah Commentary (Jewish Publication Society, 1989).

3. EMBRACING THE PEOPLE WHO DRIVE YOU CRAZY

[1]J. Richard Middleton, *The Liberating Image: The Imago Dei in Genesis 1* (Brazos Press, 2005); John H. Walton, *The Lost World of Genesis One* (InterVarsity Press, 2009).

4. WHEN BEHAVIOR IS REALLY BIOGRAPHY

[1]Daniel J. Siegel and Tina Payne Bryson, *The Whole-Brain Child: 12 Revolutionary Strategies to Nurture Your Child's Developing Mind* (Bantam Books, 2011).

[2]John Bowlby, *A Secure Base: Parent-Child Attachment and Healthy Human Development* (Basic Books, 1988).

[3]Susan David, *Emotional Agility: Get Unstuck, Embrace Change, and Thrive in Work and Life* (Avery, 2016).

5. FROM COLD WARS TO CLOSE HEARTS

[1]Kat Koppett, *Training to Imagine: Practical Improvisational Theatre Techniques to Enhance Creativity, Teamwork Leadership, and Learning* (Stylus Publishing, 2001).

[2]John M. Gottman and Nan Silver, *The Seven Principles for Making Marriage Work: A Practical Guide from the Country's Foremost Relationship Expert* (Harmony, 2015), 87.

[3]Sue Johnson, *Hold Me Tight: Seven Conversations for a Lifetime of Love* (Little, Brown, 2008).

[4]Gottman and Silver, *Seven Principles*, 23.

[5]Gottman and Silver, *Seven Principles*, 22.

[6]Gottman and Silver, *Seven Principles*, 80.

[7]Gottman and Silver, *Seven Principles*, 80-81.

[8]Thema Bryant, "Presidential Address: Psychology's Role in Addressing Oppression and Promoting Justice," *American Psychologist* 77, no. 7 (2022).

[9]Marshall B. Rosenberg, *Nonviolent Communication: A Language of Life*, 2nd ed. (PuddleDancer Press, 2003).

[10]Gottman and Silver, *Seven Principles*, 32.

6. THE ANATOMY OF DISCONNECTION

[1]John M. Gottman and Nan Silver, *The Seven Principles for Making Marriage Work: A Practical Guide from the Country's Foremost Relationship Expert* (Harmony, 2015), 32.

[2]Gottman and Silver, *Seven Principles*, 130.

[3]Gottman and Silver, *Seven Principles*.

[4]Sue Johnson, *Hold Me Tight: Seven Conversations for a Lifetime of Love* (Little, Brown, 2008).

[5]Harriet Lerner, *The Dance of Anger: A Woman's Guide to Changing the Patterns of Intimate Relationships* 2nd ed. (Harper, 2005).

7. WHY WE LOVE THE WAY WE DO

[1]Vincent J. Felitti et al., "Relationship of Childhood Abuse and Household Dysfunction to Many of the Leading Causes of Death in Adults," *American Journal of Preventive Medicine* 14, no. 4 (May 1998): 245-58.

[2]Martin H. Teicher and Jacqueline A. Samson, "Annual Research Review: Enduring Neurobiological Effects of Childhood Abuse and Neglect," *Journal of Child Psychology and Psychiatry* 57, no2.3 (2016).

[3]Bessel van der Kolk, *The Body Keeps the Score: Brain, Mind, and Body in the Healing of Trauma* (Penguin, 2014).

[4]Centers for Disease Control and Prevention, *Preventing Child Abuse and Neglect* (CDC, 2019).

[5]Bruce D. Perry and Maia Szalavitz, *The Boy Who Was Raised as a Dog: And Other Stories from a Child Psychiatrist's Notebook* (Basic Books, 2006).

[6]Van der Kolk, *The Body Keeps*, 89.

[7]Felitti et al., "Relationship of Childhood Abuse."

[8]Oluwaseun O. Adigun et al., "Abuse and Neglect," in StatPearls [Internet], updated June 12, 2023 (StatPearls Publishing, 2025), www.ncbi.nlm.nih.gov/books/NBK436015/.

[9]Steven Stosny, *You Don't Have to Take It Anymore: Turn Your Resentful, Angry, or Emotionally Abusive Relationship into a Compassionate, Loving One* (Free Press, 2005).

[10]Perry and Szalavitz, *The Boy Who Was Raised*.

[11]Felitti et al., "Relationship of Childhood Abuse."

[12]Judith Lewis Herman, *Trauma and Recovery: The Aftermath of Violence—from Domestic Abuse to Political Terror* (Basic Books, 1997).

[13]Laura van Dernoot Lipsky, *Trauma Stewardship: An Everyday Guide to Caring for Self While Caring for Others* (Berrett-Koehler Publishers, 2009).

[14]Beverly Engel, *Healing Your Emotional Self: A Powerful Program to Help You Raise Your Self-Esteem, Quiet Your Inner Critic, and Overcome Your Shame* (John Wiley & Sons, 2006).

[15]Perry and Szalavitz, *The Boy Who Was Raised*, 90.

[16]Felitti et al., "Relationship of Childhood Abuse."

[17]Paul R. Amato, "The Consequences of Divorce for Adults and Children," *Journal of Marriage and Family* 62, no. 4 (2000): 1269-87.

[18]Jude Cassidy and Phillip R. Shaver, eds., *Handbook of Attachment: Theory, Research, and Clinical Applications*, 2nd ed. (Guilford Press, 2008).

[19]Felitti et al., "Relationship of Childhood Abuse."

[20]Felitti et al., "Relationship of Childhood Abuse."